city of god

faith in the streets

SARA MILES

JERICHO
BOOKS™

New York ● Boston ● Nashville

Jericho Books
Hachette Book Group
237 Park Avenue
New York, NY 10017

www.JerichoBooks.com

The author is represented by Daniel Literary Group, Nashville, Tennessee

Printed in the United States of America

RRD-C

First edition: February 2014
10 9 8 7 6 5 4 3 2 1

Jericho Books is an imprint of Hachette Book Group, Inc.
The Jericho Books name and logo are trademarks of Hachette Book Group, Inc.

The Hachette Speakers Bureau provides a wide range of authors for speaking events. To find out more, go to www.HachetteSpeakersBureau.com or call (866) 376-6591.

The publisher is not responsible for websites (or their content) that are not owned by the publisher.

ISBN: 9781455547319

LCCN: 2013953948

for Mark Pritchard
in memory of Cris Gutierrez

Author's Note

Since 2010, I've been part of a group offering ashes outdoors on Ash Wednesday in San Francisco's Mission District. This book mostly follows my experiences during one day, Ash Wednesday, 2012; given the hundreds of encounters, though, some of my notes and observations from other years may be mixed in.

I've changed details about individuals in some cases to protect privacy when requested, and I've used pseudonyms (first names only) for a few people in this book; otherwise, people are identified by their actual first and last names. I fact-checked interviews, as well as the conversations I wrote down from memory; any errors in reporting are my own.

Introduction

About fourteen years ago, I took my first communion. I hadn't known—in fact, hadn't remotely considered—that I was looking for God. I didn't believe in God: I was just poking my head into an interesting-looking building to see what was going on. Over the next decade, buoyed by the promise that a knocked-on door will be opened, I spent a lot of time in churches, seeking—and sometimes even finding—God.

If you want to find God, look inside a church. That doesn't seem unreasonable to most Christians, or even to unbelievers like the one I was. But it isn't the whole story.

St. Gregory of Nyssa Episcopal Church in San Francisco, where I took that bread, was the place I first encountered prayer, the Bible, sacraments—and other Christians. It's where I was baptized, where I was taught about the faith, and where, inspired by communion, I started a food pantry, set up right around the same altar. It became the place I worked, as a lay preacher, pastor, and liturgist; the place I wrote about, and a portal into all kinds of other church communities.

And then, just as I was getting used to the idea of working inside the Church, for what my priest friend Paul calls "the company" and my pastor friend Nadia calls "the Jesus business," I was driven outside by the hot breath of the Holy Spirit. Back where I started: outside the building and looking for God.

In the years I've been a Christian, a lot of other Christians have left the building, too: or, more accurately, they have found ways to encounter God outside the boundaries of what happens inside churches on Sunday mornings. Church, in the sense of a discrete, set-aside ritual space run by set-aside religious professionals, is perhaps weaker as an institution in the United States than it's ever been. While religious fluidity and denomination-switching among Christians are increasing—and the numbers of non-Christian believers are growing—a significant number of Americans have just stopped participating in religion, with fully a quarter of all adults under thirty saying they have no religious affiliation at all. Across the country, mainline Protestant congregations are consistently getting older and smaller, with many of them laying off staff and closing their doors.

And yet there's a growing network of "unhoused" congregations meeting outdoors to serve people who live on the streets; all kinds of new public rituals of blessing (of bicycles, of pets, of backpacks) are taking place in parks and on sidewalks; there's a reinvigorated interest in outdoor processions for feast days and for Holy Week; there are hundreds of churches offering ashes outside for Ash Wednesday.

This book isn't about how to fix or save or reinvent church; it's not a manual for doing outdoor liturgies or a polemic against indoor worship. It's simply the story of how I began to discover faith in the streets of my city—especially through the liturgies of Ash Wednesday, with their recognition of common mortality and their call for repentance and change.

While God is remarkably flexible about showing up anywhere—in the desert, in a manger, in a burning bush, or in a prison cell—the eyes of my own faith see the most on urban streets. For me, paradise is a garden, but heaven is a city.

Though prophets tend to describe the heavenly city with fantasy-Barbie imagery that leans heavily on golden robes, sparkling fountains, and precious stones, the actual urban place I've lived in for more than twenty years—the Mission District of San Francisco—has changed my view of heaven. As the Mission painfully keeps shaping my Christianity, I begin to see how the new Jerusalem might look less like a pious Disneyland and more like—well, like the "New Jerusalem" bodega run by Syrian Christians that I trudge past on my way to work, its dingy pink front plastered over with Miller beer signs, its enthusiastic, unshaven owner waving and smiling each new day as he opens the door to welcome in a straggling, polyglot parade of schoolkids, nurses, winos, and day laborers.

I begin to see that city-ness, not necessarily prettiness, might be a characteristic sign of heaven. Sexier and more beautiful than Eden, the city of God is a crowded, busy place jammed with languages and peoples, including the ones who argue incessantly with one another. A place so mixed, so layered, and apparently impure that it proclaims a love vaster than humans can come up with on our own. A place as surprising and generous as the sheet full of formerly unclean food in the Book of Acts that turns Peter from heaven's gatekeeper into its dazzled servant.

In the city of God, a river of life flows from the single source of holiness, while a bent street tree, cracking open the sidewalk with its tough roots, offers its leaves for the healing of all the nations.

The city of God. Here it is. Heaven, on earth.

city of god

chapter one

It was completely dark when I woke up on the morning of Ash Wednesday, 2012, and very still. The predawn streets of my San Francisco neighborhood, the Mission, were empty, and on the corner a stand of blooming almond trees gleamed white against a white house that seemed to levitate over the dirty gray sidewalk.

I got in my car and headed toward St. Gregory of Nyssa Episcopal Church, about a mile and a half away in Potrero Hill, where I was working on staff as a lay minister. We would be holding three services that day: two at St. Gregory's—at seven in the morning and seven in the evening—and one outdoors, in the afternoon, offering ashes on the streets of the Mission. I planned to take part in them all.

On Tuesday afternoon, I'd spent hours taking down

all the gold lamé and bright white banners we used to celebrate Epiphany, the season of light, and draped the worship space with the somber mudcloth of Lent, rough brown fabric from Africa stamped with black geometric lines. On stands at the entryway, I'd placed icons of a sorrowing Virgin Mary and Jesus; I also set out bowls of beeswax candles in front of an icon showing the prophet Amos unfurling a scroll: "Let justice roll down like rivers," its gold lettering proclaimed. There was another, of the mad, dreadlocked John the Baptist ranting about vipers and coming tribulations. St. Gregory's rector, my friend Paul Fromberg, was an iconographer himself, and had given me instructions on choosing the right images for Lent.

"Prophets, always appropriate," he said. "And Mary, of course. She goes anywhere."

At around seven Tuesday evening, I'd finally finished. I left the church, heading down Potrero Hill back toward the Mission, making a stop on the way at the San Francisco General Hospital to pick up my wife Martha, who worked as a nurse in the wound clinic. She came to the curb wearing green scrubs and slid into the front seat with a sigh. "Long day," she said. It was always a long day.

We were both ready to crash, but we'd been cajoled

into attending a "really important" community meeting organized by a Chicano activist whose kids had gone to elementary school long ago with our daughter. "One hour," I promised Martha as we parked behind the little Spanish-language Lutheran church near our home. "Then it's bedtime. I have to be at work by six tomorrow to set up with Mark for the early Ash Wednesday service." Martha, a secular Jew, didn't always keep track of the Christian calendar, but she was patient. "Fine with me," she said.

Inside the messy meeting room, our friend was holding forth, chipper as always. He sported a ponytail and a scraggly beard now, and he wore a little crucifix around his neck. There were a few other people from our block, including Ricardo, an eager organizer I'd known since he was eleven years old, and some union guys who had ordered in greasy cheese pizza for everyone. We got there a little late, so the agenda wasn't totally clear. Ricardo wanted to talk about stopping a chain supermarket from moving into the Mission. A neighbor whose name I'd never learned, a squat, surly older man, wanted to talk about punishing the wicked delinquents who disrespected private property and threw garbage on the streets. I wanted to leave early. "*Tengo que trabajar bien tempranito en la mañana*," I explained to the group apologetically. "*Miercoles de ceniza*, gotta work early tomorrow, it's Ash Wednesday."

"Oh, man, *miercoles de ceniza?*" said the organizer. "Wow, already? I didn't remember. Ricardo, let's finish up and send out minutes. Okay, Sara, *mujer, nos vemos*, see you soon, call me."

"Ashes to ashes," said Martha when we got home. She kissed me. "I'm really exhausted. How early do you have to be at work again?"

It wasn't quite six in the morning as I drove toward St. Gregory's, sipping coffee from a chipped mug. The streets seemed quiet for a Wednesday, and most of the little corner stores in my neighborhood were closed up tight behind their metal gates, though I could see two men already at work inside a small Mexican bakery, lifting trays of rolls and pastries out of the oven. Passing through the Mission and up a steep hill, I came down over the crest into Potrero Hill, along a street that suddenly yielded a long, wide view of the city and the Oakland port, with tanker ships weightlessly suspended over glassy silver water, and to the northeast the lights of the Bay Bridge. I parked by the brewery across the street from St. Gregory's and walked up to the church's heavy, carved front doors. They were shut, and the turreted, wood-shingled building looked dark.

St. Gregory's doors open directly into a spacious rotunda, unfurnished except for a round wooden altar table for communion at the center, and a monumental icon of life-size dancing saints painted on the walls above. Beyond a thicket of standing Ethiopian Orthodox silver crosses, there's a seating area where people listen to Scripture and sermons. Outside, through tall doors, you can glimpse the waters of the baptismal font, carved from a huge stone boulder and set in the narrow, ivy-covered side of a hill.

Many visitors to St. Gregory's, drawn by its reputation for "experimental" liturgy, assume we must be a sort of modern, hippie, anything-goes kind of congregation. In fact, St. Gregory's is unabashedly old-school—just not in the familiar nineteenth-century Anglophile style of most Episcopal parishes. There's a lot of color: printed silks draped everywhere, pink and gold and bright blue vestments, even sparkly liturgical umbrellas. There's a lot of

Jesus, and of Mary, and during the week, at the food pantry, a lot of potatoes and onions pile up around their beautiful images in the rotunda. People move through the space chanting ancient hymns; they offer spontaneous prayers aloud, kiss the Gospel book fervently, dance beneath the saints around the altar. They paint icons, write music, bake bread, lay sweaty hands on one another in blessing. Worship at St. Gregory's is meant to offer a full-body experience of God, not just chatter *about* God; it isn't always comfortable, but it seldom feels rote.

I punched in my alarm code and entered the church, pausing to touch the icon of Mary. A single light was on in the kitchen: Mark Pritchard was already there, pulling cabinet doors open. He was wearing black jeans and a sweatshirt, and had a takeout cup of coffee on the counter. "Okay, I give up," Mark greeted me, a little crabbily. "Where are the ashes? I mean, isn't it *Ash* Wednesday?"

Twenty years before, when I moved to the Mission, Mark was one of the first people I met there. He seemed like just another cool bisexual artist who stayed up late, roaming from dive bars to dark parks to Red Dora's lesbian café, performing Carpenters songs with ironic aplomb on his dorky little Casio keyboard and holding down an office temp job.

Mark was a prolific writer whose stories were funny, insightful, and wildly pornographic; he was a hardworking editor who, with his brilliant lover Cris Gutierrez, published the underground zine *Frighten the Horses.* He was a loyal and helpful friend, always ready to cheer up a depressed writer or ferry a man with AIDS to the doctor or have coffee with lost souls like me, in between helping Cris recover from back surgeries or running endless errands for her elderly, nutty Salvadoran aunt.

Cris and Mark, former high school teachers in the Mission, were also activists: she volunteered with immigrants seeking asylum and tenants fighting eviction. Mark helped start Street Patrol, a Guardian Angels–inspired group that marched through the streets of the Castro at night to deter gay-bashings, decked out in leather jackets and hot pink berets. I'd joined up one sunny afternoon in Dolores Park, where Mark was training people how to get hit without getting hurt. Strong and stocky, with buzz-cut orange hair, ACT-UP stickers all over his jacket, and a tongue piercing, Mark looked like any tough white Mission queer but sounded like the kindest gym teacher on the planet. "Hup!" he said encouragingly, as I got knocked down by another street patroller and rolled over. "Upsy-daisy, good try! Let's do it one more time."

Mark, to my great surprise, turned out to be a practicing Christian: a Lutheran, in fact, who attended a steepled church every Sunday, where he sat in a wooden pew and sang earnest, old-fashioned hymns. At the time, I didn't know anyone else who was a Christian: San Francisco, with one of the lowest rates of church attendance of any city in the nation, fit my own religious profile perfectly. I hadn't gone to church as a child; I drew a blank when it came to Bible stories, Sunday school, Christmas Eve services, or songs about Jesus. Mark didn't talk about any of that, though, so I mostly considered his faith just one more quirky preference, like a fondness for corsets, of no particular import in the overall scheme of things.

Yet when, years later, I stumbled into St. Gregory's—whether by accident or by the grace of the Holy Spirit, but in any case utterly without premeditation—it was Mark I turned to, desperate for some basic instruction. I'd been blindsided by my unplanned first communion, turned upside down by eating that bread and drinking that wine and finding God, whom I didn't believe in, alive in my mouth. It was almost like being taken down by the Street Patrol girl with a black belt in aikido. What happened? I wanted to ask Mark. What the hell was *that* about? *Now* what?

I read Simone Weil's warning about conversion: a Jew and leftist intellectual in France during the Second World War, she had not planned to find Jesus, either, and though a hundred times more learned than I, had been equally alarmed about the implications when she did. "If there is a God," she wrote, "it is not an insignificant fact, but something that requires a radical rethinking of *every little thing*. Your knowledge of God can't be considered as one fact among many. You have to bring all the other facts into line with the fact of God."

And so, clumsily, I tried. Mark was, as usual, glad to be helpful: not particularly fired up about my conversion but mercifully matter-of-fact. He'd never minded my lack of religion: Cris wasn't a believer, and his performance-artist, stripper, countercultural friends were generally shocked to learn he went to church—though, as Mark pointed out, "If I said I went to the Zen Center, nobody would think twice."

Mark brought me to services at his church, St. Francis Lutheran, where a friendly lesbian pastor in a rainbow stole preached, sort of boringly, about social justice. Mark accompanied me to St. Gregory's, the place where I'd tasted God, and gamely joined in that congregation's dense, a cappella harmonies. He lent me a couple of books by Thomas Merton and continued to show me his dirty stories. When, after a year or so of anguished struggle, I decided to give up and be baptized at St. Gregory's, Mark offered to serve as my godfather. His hair, no longer orange, was graying a bit at the temples, but he had the same reassuring solidity. "Will you, by your prayers and witness, help this person to grow into the full stature of Christ?" the priest asked Mark, who was standing next to me at the outdoor baptismal font, wearing a nice blazer for the occasion. "With God's help, I will," he said firmly.

Within a few years, Mark, though retaining his right to belt out gloomy Lutheran hymns whenever he felt like it, had started to worship at St. Gregory's, too. It had become my home church and the rich center of my new life. I started a food pantry at St. Gregory's, offering free groceries to hundreds of families in a sort of free farmer's market set up right around the altar; I got involved in planning liturgies and began preaching, and eventually was hired part-time by Paul to direct pastoral care. By 2012, Mark and I were both regularly serving as lay leaders at the Eucharist on Sundays; every weekday at eight we sang morning prayer together, chanting Psalms or sitting companionably in silence beneath the icons, old friends in a new place.

"Here," I said, opening the cabinet where we kept tea bags, sugar packets, and miscellaneous paper goods, and handed Mark the ashes. We'd prepared them from those great triumphal palm fronds used in St. Gregory's procession on Palm Sunday, at the beginning of last year's Holy Week, when we hailed Jesus as king then howled for his execution. Mark had organized a group of machete-wielding friends to cut palm branches from a parishioner's yard, strapped them to the top of his station wagon with bungee cords, and driven through a car wash to rinse them off before hoisting them up in the church. They were beautiful: huge prehistoric branches that swayed from the high rafters and doorways of St. Gregory's. We left a couple up through Easter, then dragged them out into a corner of the backyard, where they were dumped into an unsightly pile with some tree trimmings and brush until the summer, when Mark and I got around to hacking the branches up into little pieces, composting most of them and finally burning a handful. Palms are extraordinarily hard to set on fire, and it took several tries, but at last we got about half a cup of ashes, which we pushed through a sieve into two small ceramic bowls and then stuck in a corner of the kitchen to save for Ash Wednesday.

Ashes are what a fire cannot burn. What's left over after a fire, or from a life. Now Mark and I carried the ashes out into the dark church, along with two round loaves of fresh bread and a glass flagon of sweet, sticky wine for communion. I placed music books on chairs and marked the book of readings at the lectern: Prophets, always appropriate. Near the doors, we laid bowls of warm water on a table with some folded towels, so people could choose to wash the ashes off their faces before leaving church, following Jesus' admonition to "beware of practicing your piety before others in order to be seen by them."

After we lit the oil lamps hanging over the altar, it was almost six thirty. St. Gregory's music director and cantor, Sanford Dole, had already slipped in and quickly headed to the seating area where he'd open the service with chanting. Mark and I went to the vestry to get dressed in the long, floor-sweeping black cassocks I decided would signify our appropriately serious Lenten attitude. I tucked away the little Virgin of Guadalupe medallion I always wore, and was reaching inside Mark's cassock to fasten his collar button for him, when Paul strode in, far too energetically for the hour, and corrected my ignorant mistake in his authoritative rector voice. "No! White!" said Paul. "Always wear white when we're celebrating the Eucharist! It means resurrection! Change your clothes!"

Like Mark, Paul was originally from Houston. A big, strong, Jesus-loving gay man, Paul's constant wisecracks couldn't entirely obscure his enormous intellect or his faith. His memory was unnervingly good: Paul could rattle off multiple hymn verses from the conservative Church of Christ he grew up in, entire Anglican litanies, and big chunks of 1980s television shows, word for word.

"Let us prepare ourselves for spiritual efforts," he pronounced grandly, as he went over to the racks of vestments and started flipping through the priests' stoles. I knew Paul was quoting from some part of our Ash Wednesday liturgy, but it wasn't until he started humming that I caught on and remembered it was from an Orthodox chant.

"*Let us begin the fast with joy,* something something *armor of light?*" I asked. "That's it," said Paul, picking out a brown mudcloth stole to wear. "*And lay aside the works of darkness and put on the armor of light.*"

"Nice," said Mark. We swapped our cassocks for white albs. As we straightened them out, Paul handed us three-ring binders holding the final scripts he'd prepared. He looked pleased.

"Ash Wednesday is really good for the church," Paul said. I looked at my friend and thought how difficult it must be for him, sometimes, to contain his fervent faith inside the conventions of the institution. "Not just for individuals. The other three hundred sixty-four days of the year, we think we're fine. We think we're not going to die, if we just tweak our music or our coffee hour or the associate rector's new program. On Ash Wednesday we have to realize, we have to *corporately* realize, that we are completely out of control."

I peeked out from the vestry into the seating area of the church. Sanford, a tall, trim white man with a high forehead, was already in the cantor's chair. The church used no instruments in worship, but Sanford had an amazing ability to coax full, beautiful harmonies from nonprofessional singers, even those who couldn't read music and insisted they couldn't sing. "I just love the music out of them," he'd explained once. With him, waiting for the service to begin, were twenty or so people in rows of chairs facing each other across a narrow platform. Most were sitting quietly, though Vik Slen, a blond seminarian, was on his knees, praying. There were a few strangers, too, whom I'd never seen before at St. Gregory's. I wondered what impulse or habit or deep need had driven them, so early in the morning, to find a building where they could observe Ash Wednesday.

"Comrade Miles?" said Paul, interrupting my reverie. He handed Mark a deacon's candle and picked up his heavy presider's cross. "Chop chop, it's almost seven."

chapter two

As the three of us walked in, Sanford and the congregation rose to their feet and began singing a Russian hymn. *"Come heavenly comforter,"* it began, *"and spirit of truth, blowing everywhere and filling all things."* The tune was so lovely I could almost forget the harsh irony nestled in the words: heavenly comfort is not comforting at all. Heavenly comfort, rather, is *truth*, which blows away human fantasies that we can live forever, control everything, or fake our lives before God. *"Treasury of blessings, and giver of life, come and abide in us."* And the truth is that God, who smashed the temple of stone, abides in the bodies of *all* people, fills *all* things—making no distinction whatsoever between strangers and neighbors. If I considered my own struggles to live honestly with others on my block, even with my friends and family, I had to wonder how wise it really was to pray for the spirit of truth to come.

The song ended. "Let us begin the fast with joy," Paul chanted as candles flickered in the dim church, illuminating his grave blue eyes and the faces of the people standing in front of him.

I picked up one bowl of ashes and handed the other to Mark, who stepped forward. "Let us kneel before the God who made us," Mark told the congregation. And then he and I and everyone in the room got down, some fully prostrated and others on their knees, and waited, in silence, for a full three minutes. I could hear the people near me breathing. And when Sanford rang a little bell we all heaved ourselves up; then Mark and I began the imposition of ashes. One by one, each person took a bowl of ashes, turned toward a neighbor and marked the cross, slowly, on a forehead, passed the bowl and bent to receive the same sign.

"Remember you are dust," we told one another. "And to dust you will return."

The liturgy continued with an admonition from the prophet Joel: "Return to me with all your heart," it began, "with fasting, with weeping, and with mourning." Then a song of Isaiah's: "Your holy cities are a wilderness," the prophet warned his sinful people. "Now pour down, you heavens, from above: and let the skies rain down righteousness."

Ash Wednesday's emphasis on catastrophe could be a bit off-putting. Massacres, weeping, swords, desolation: these aren't the kinds of events the Church usually celebrates. Jews might be familiar with making liturgy out of catastrophe, but Jews live, and pray, close to the experience of collective suffering. Christians, more prone to personalize faith, tend to look away, keeping pain private and liturgy uplifting.

But on Ash Wednesday we have to kneel together and repent.

The prayers of penitence at St. Gregory's were less detailed than those from the Book of Common Prayer used in Episcopal churches, which begin: "Create and make in us new and contrite hearts, that we, worthily lamenting our sins and acknowledging our wretchedness, may obtain of you, the God of all mercy, perfect remission and forgiveness..." The Book of Common Prayer has worshippers confess aloud a daunting catalog of sins: "All our past unfaithfulness: the pride, hypocrisy, and impatience of our lives; our self-indulgent appetites and ways and our exploitation of other people; our anger at our own frustration and our envy of those more fortunate than ourselves; our intemperate love of worldly goods and comfort; our dishonesty in daily life and work; our negligence in prayer and worship, and our failure to commend the faith that is in us." Then, just to cover all bases, there's "our blindness to human need and suffering, our indifference to injustice and cruelty; all false judgments, uncharitable thoughts toward our neighbors, and our prejudice and contempt toward those who differ from us."

While working on St. Gregory's liturgy for Ash Wednesday, Paul and I argued a bit about the challenges of collective confession. "Doesn't it kind of let me off the hook," I protested, "to say *we* have wasted your creation, blah blah, *we* have been snide, blah blah, *we* have failed at whatever? Shouldn't I have to consider my own actual sins and look at exactly what it is I've personally done and am ready to repent of?"

"Ah," said Paul. "That would be the sin of pride, thinking that your wickedness is so different from others'."

Paul decided to conclude the prayers simply, "Grant us to see our own sins"; a request I thought as risky as asking for the spirit of truth to come. How closely did I really want to look? "Grant us to see our own sins, and not judge those of our sisters and brothers."

As we prayed and sang and moved through the service, a more nuanced picture of Ash Wednesday's themes emerged: repentance, yes, but with less "wretchedness" and more forgiveness.

Repentance, in Christian practice, is not a psychological or an emotional process. "Feelings," Paul declared once when I brought him some intractable problem with a troubled parishioner, "are stupid." I thought he must be joking, but Paul insisted. "Jesus doesn't care if you feel guilty. Jesus wants you to change."

Neither is repentance about simply saying you're sorry. "That's just apology," explained Paul, "which is about etiquette. Repentance is about rebirth. It means putting on your big-girl panties and facing the world to do things differently."

Though the Bible describes people trying to demonstrate their sorrow before God through rituals like fasting, wearing sackcloth, and pouring ashes on their heads, prophets like the ones we read aloud on Ash Wednesday insist these acts do not constitute repentance unless there's a real change of behavior.

"Is *this* the kind of fast I have chosen," God demands, in Isaiah's account, "one day for lying on sackcloth and ashes? Is *that* what you call a fast, a day acceptable to the

Lord? Is not this the kind of fasting I have chosen: to loose the chains of injustice and untie the cords of the yoke, to set the oppressed free and break every yoke? Is it not to share your food with the hungry and to provide the poor wanderer with shelter—when you see the naked, to clothe him, and not to turn away from your own flesh and blood?"

Repentance means turning toward other human beings, our own flesh and blood, whenever they're oppressed, hungry, or imprisoned; it means acting with compassion instead of indifference. It means turning away, "fasting," from any of the little and big things that can keep us from God—drugs, religion, busy-ness, video games, lies—and accepting the divine embrace with all our hearts. Repentance requires paying attention to others, and learning to love, even a little bit, what God loves so much: the whole screwed-up world, this holy city, the people God created to be his own.

The sanctuary was brighter now; almost imperceptibly, the sun had risen while we were praying and it was plain day. I glanced at Mark, who was sitting with his back straight, gazing calmly at the smoke curling from the bowl of incense. Whenever I got too carried away with fussing about vestments and candles and readings, I remembered how useful it had been when Mark taught us to get knocked down in Street Patrol: the reality of landing on my ass in the dirt overrode any more existential fears. This service did the same thing, reminding me not to over-spiritualize the problem of mortality. Ash Wednesday was calling me back to worship God with my whole body—lungs, thumb, knees, eyes, tongue—and to admit that body's inevitable failure. And it reminded me that I was no different in my flesh from any other human being.

I looked around at the members of the congregation, their faces smudged with ashes. The marks reminded me of the cross of sticky ointment a priest had sealed my forehead with at baptism, and of the mark God put on the forehead of the fratricidal Cain to place him outside human judgment. We were all so messed up.

"The worst thing we can imagine is that we're made out of dirt and going to die," Paul said to me once. "But when we say it aloud, we discover the worst thing isn't the last thing. The last thing is forgiveness."

"We'll go up to the Table in step, singing 'Eternal Lord of Love,'" I announced at the end of the readings and silences and prayers. Sanford gave the pitch and page number for the hymn. "Three steps forward, one step back," he instructed. "Put your hand on the shoulder of the person in front of you." I could feel Mark's hand on me, firm and warm, as we stepped off, singing about death and springtime, and wound our way around the altar.

We stood closely together at the Table as Paul sang the Eucharistic prayer, "The Great Thanksgiving of Cain Our Father." Mark and I helped break the loaves of home-made bread into little pieces and passed chalices of wine around so people could share communion with one another. Then Paul lifted his big hands and chanted: "Holy God, our lives are laid open before you. Rescue us from the chaos of sin; bring us healing and make us whole."

Finally came the section of the liturgy Paul had developed, based on the Orthodox Forgiveness Vespers, that he referred to as "the Virginia reel of forgiveness." As a tepid morning sun glanced off the icons of Simone Weil and King David dancing above us, Sanford began to chant quietly. "Now is the hour of repentance," he sang. Mark instructed everyone to gather in a circle, form pairs, then move slowly around the rotunda to face each other member in turn, pausing to say, "Forgive me, a sinner" and to hear back, "God forgives you. Forgive me, a sinner." I looked at the middle-aged woman in front of me, someone I hardly knew, even after six years. I hadn't exactly avoided her, but neither had I gone out of my way to connect with or pay attention to her. "Forgive me, a sinner," I said, suddenly aware of all my stupid mistakes, minor cruelties, and real betrayals. "God forgives you," the woman said. She took a breath. "Forgive me, a sinner." "God forgives you," I told her, and moved on to the next person.

Mark was helping steer someone who'd got mixed up; a mother was bending to ask her son for forgiveness; Paul was touching each of his parishioners in turn. Nearby, I saw an older white couple, members of St. Gregory's who'd been married for years, holding hands as they looked steadily, without speaking, into each other's faces. Sanford lifted his voice over our shamble of confessions and absolutions, the haunting minor tone echoing through the rotunda. "*Let us lay aside the works of darkness and put on the armor of light, that passing through the fast as through a great sea we may reach the resurrection.*" "Forgive me, a sinner," said the old man, finally. His wife gazed at him. "God forgives you," she said. "Forgive me, a sinner."

Paul watched as we all finished moving through the room and then lifted his hands for the final prayer. *"Lord,"* he sang tenderly, *"now let your servant depart in peace, according to your word, for my eyes have seen your salvation."*

chapter three

I was in the kitchen with Paul, a little past eight, scrubbing the ashes off my fingers with a dirty washcloth, after Sanford and the last morning parishioner had left. The door opened and Mark came over to fetch me, sounding worried. "It's Mr. Claws," he said. "He looks really bad."

"Shit," I said. I'd totally forgotten to remind Mr. Claws that, because of Ash Wednesday services, we wouldn't be holding morning prayer, and here he was, as usual, expecting to see us. "Do you have any cash for him? I've just got a few dollars."

"No, I think he's in trouble," said Mark. "Come see."

Every Wednesday, Mark and I would greet one of our regulars at morning prayer: an elderly, raspy-voiced Creole man whom we referred to, privately, as Mr. Claws, for the horrific uncut yellowed fingernails that curled over his arthritic hands. Mr. Claws was a steady weekly visitor, who carried a torn backpack and would flee into the chapel bathroom to "wash up and change for work" the instant we let him in; there, he'd swap one cheap windbreaker for another and emerge with wet hair to sit with us in the quiet church. He didn't seem to be able to read, though he always held the morning prayer booklet in front of him through the whole service, making mumbling noises as we sang. I couldn't believe he had a job—Mr. Claws looked to be at least twenty years past retirement age—though he invariably asked Mark or me for seven dollars for bus and train fare to get to work.

Mark listened patiently and actually gave Mr. Claws raises. But if it was my turn to be approached I'd often quickly hand Mr. Claws a few bills, trying to cut off the rambling, deceitful stories—sometimes he said he had a job in a hotel restaurant downtown, sometimes out in the East Bay. Each Wednesday there'd be an even longer and more elaborate version of the same inept scam. "Darling, I gotta get to work," he'd say urgently, grabbing at my arm with his shaky, not-too-clean hands. "I've got an extra shift this week, I used to borrow a car but the engine died, my boss don't want anybody but me to do it..."

27

If I went out of town and missed a weekly payment he'd scold me. "I was worried about you," he'd growl in his thick Louisiana accent. "Where *was* you?"

I didn't object to giving Mr. Claws money. I always gave money to anyone who asked me, on principle: it made my life simpler not to have to worry about who deserved what, and as long as I had some cash in my pocket I didn't mind sharing it. But working in a church means entertaining a steady parade of people stopping by to "talk to the pastor" and ask for money. A few of them are direct, but most, as if following some unwritten script for mendicants, are roundabout and fawning as they deliver their stilted performances: *So sorry to bother you, I'm just in town visiting my sister, and someone stole my wallet; Pastor, I know you have a good heart, I need to get just a gallon of gas, I'm on my way to my grandfather's funeral; Ma'am, I hate to bother you, but I have asthma and my medication ran out, and now I have to go to a new pharmacy and they said it would cost thirteen dollars more than usual, and my little daughter's in school and I had to give her lunch money this morning, I hate to ask, but I thought the church might be able to loan me something so I can fill the prescription, oh, God bless you . . .* It was not only irritating to be constantly interrupted, but insulting to be the object of such transparent attempts at manipulation: just because I was a Christian, it didn't mean I was an idiot.

But one Wednesday morning when Mark was away I showed up a little late, and as I was busily unlocking the church doors Mr. Claws, who'd been waiting outside since God knows when, launched right in. "Oh, darling, I'm glad you're finally here, the train fare went up again and I'm trying to get to work…"

I interrupted him. "Listen," I said. "I'll give you the money, okay, but please don't lie to me, I just don't want to hear it this morning." I pushed past Mr. Claws and lit the candles, and as I looked back impatiently over my shoulder I saw him standing there crumpled: a solitary old man with no job anymore, only the memory of one, who'd been showing up on schedule, dressing for work, and praying with us, trying to act out the story that kept his sense of meaning alive.

Now, though, Mr. Claws was leaning bent over against the chapel doorway. His brown skin was a dull gray, and his breath was uneven; there was an awful smell coming from his pants. "He really can't stand up," Mark said. "I think he should go to the emergency room."

Mr. Claws just croaked indistinctly when I asked if he

was okay, and he started explaining, very slowly. "Sorry I'm, I'm late," he said, his growl even lower than usual. "But the power went out this morning. Got up and then it was all black. Couldn't see anything." I took his arm. "Fell and hit my head," he said, and again, wondering, "Darling, the power just went out."

One of his long, hornlike fingernails was broken, and he couldn't seem to keep his balance. How, I thought, did Mr. Claws possibly find his way here? Where did he live, and with whom? Could it be that St. Gregory's was his only home, that we were his only family? "If we call 911 the ambulance will take him, and he'll be alone and scared," reasoned Mark. "I can drive him to the General and drop him at the emergency room, but I can't stay with him, I have to go to work."

"Okay," I said, "I can be down there within an hour." I went back to the kitchen to find Paul, who was going to remain at St. Gregory's all day, and told him my plans. Then I scribbled my phone number on a card for Mr. Claws, and Mark helped the old man walk out the door, holding his arm graciously, and drove him down the hill from the church to the San Francisco General Hospital, in the Mission.

San Francisco General Hospital is *in* but not entirely *of* the Mission. Located on 23rd Street, it's in the flats below Potrero Hill, close to the freeways. Its emergency department and trauma center draw the mortally ill and wounded from all over the Bay Area; its AIDS and psych wards serve sufferers from far beyond the boundaries of the immediate neighborhood; a research and training center for the University of California, it is virtually the only hospital in the city that provides full care for indigent patients. The General is a place of almost unbearable realness, whose staff workers pride themselves on being able to care for every person who stumbles through its scuffed, dented doors. "Oh," I can imagine a doctor saying calmly to the umpteenth patient of the night, "oh, so you have HIV and heart disease and a heroin habit and one leg and a touch of bipolar disorder? And you're pregnant? No problem, let me just take a look at that little bullet wound in your gut first." But the swagger and machismo that attach to such extreme urban medicine, with its frequent flyers and budget cuts and hellishly complicated cases, can yield, surprisingly often, to compassion. At the General, the longtime staff—the lifers—tend to care more, not less.

I arrived in San Francisco in 1989 pregnant and broke, having left my job as a war reporter in El Salvador to relocate to what a friend called "the northernmost city in Latin America." Like so many other immigrants, I wound up at the county hospital—not for free health care, in my case, but to get coupons from a government program that would provide me and the baby with milk, cereal, and juice. The WIC office, on the ground floor of an old-fashioned brick building, was an inefficient and friendly place, full of women lugging toddlers and chatting with each other in many languages.

Many years later, when Martha started to work there in an outpatient clinic, I'd come to know the General better. One of her co-workers, a tall, chic black woman with a tattoo on her neck reading "JOHN 3:16," had jumped up the first time I stopped by to see Martha on a break. "Oh!" she nearly shouted, apparently delighted by the fact that her Jewish colleague's lesbian partner was a Christian preacher. "I've heard all about you!" She gave me a big hug. "Give me a call any time, any time at all you want to talk about Jesus. Bless you!"

But not everyone was that friendly. The mustachioed

white sheriff posted at the door to the emergency department examined me coolly when I arrived looking for Mr. Claws. It was not even nine in the morning, and the waiting room had already acquired a collection of nodding junkies slumped in plastic chairs or queuing up for the bathroom. A couple of little kids pressed their faces against a vending machine, as if the sheer intensity of their desire could make packets of Cheetos emerge.

"Talk to her," the sheriff said, nodding in the direction of a young woman at the reception desk wearing scrubs and a smear of ashes on her forehead. I gave her Mr. Claws's real name and asked if I could go in to see him. "Family?" she asked.

"No," I said. "His pastor."

It turned out that while I'd been at the church straightening up after the morning service, Mr. Claws had already been seen, discharged, and given a prescription to fill. The General's pharmacy was notoriously backlogged, so I figured there was plenty of time to track down the emergency department social worker while he waited to get his pills. She was harried and friendly, but didn't have much to tell me: they'd quickly diagnosed a urinary-tract infection that tended to make elderly patients confused, and after pushing some fluids and antibiotics into him the doctors had sent Mr. Claws on his way. "Do you know where he lives?" the social worker asked me. "He told us he's in Redwood City, which is San Mateo County, so he'll have to get follow-up care there."

I had no idea where Mr. Claws lived; if he had an apartment, a hotel room, or a hiding place on the streets. He'd never given me or Mark an address, didn't have a phone, and never mentioned any relatives.

The social worker sighed. "He made a mess, so we showered him off and got him some new pants," she said. "He can get his prescription here. But that's all we can do: really he should have someone looking in on him."

She walked me down the narrow hallway, where patients lay on gurneys, moaning or sleeping or staring with dull amazement at the IVs in their arms and the blood on their gowns. Exhausted young residents wove past family members and orderlies and a couple of cops keeping watch over a prisoner.

Here and there, I spotted someone marked with ashes. I wondered why, if you worked at the General, you'd want to participate in this particular ritual: how could you possibly need another reminder of mortality? But my friend Will Hocker, an Episcopal priest who ran the interfaith Sojourn Chaplaincy at the hospital, said that in his experience very few doctors were comfortable talking about death with patients—or with each other. "It's just not considered right," he said. "I did all this research showing better outcomes when palliative care was introduced earlier, but doctors hate to even bring up mortality. The culture of a hospital is to say, 'we can fix it,' and so saying, 'you're going to die' is crazy."

Will had a lined, expressive face, and told me once he'd never baptized a live baby, just stillborn ones; his priesthood tended to happen in the unadorned hallways and nurses' stations and waiting rooms where it was clear nothing could be fixed. Will, who had lain near death himself from complications of AIDS, knew the difference between heavenly comfort and comfort, and he always leaned into the former. "The truth is the truth," he said with a shrug.

In 2010, the year we first held an Ash Wednesday liturgy on Mission Street, Will organized a morning service at the General and invited staff and families. "Some were Catholics, and it was a familiar part of their practice," he said. "But we also had people who weren't necessarily conversant in Christian ritual. I think they sort of realized it was an invitation to acknowledge limits. To bow down in public and say, I'm not in charge;

I'm not going to live forever. And they were really, *really* interested in that."

The chapel was under construction then, so Will set up folding chairs in an empty conference room on the inpatient psychiatric floor. I was eager to see one more way of doing this ritual, so I brought over ashes from St. Gregory's after the early service. About twenty nurses and medical assistants—either coming off night shifts, or getting ready for the day's work—were gathered. "Eternal Lord of love, behold your church," we sang together, the hymn sounding muffled and flat in the windowless, low-ceilinged room. There was silence.

"Let us kneel before the God who made us," Will said, his voice weary, and everyone knelt together on the badly worn floor. "Almighty God," Will prayed, "you created us out of the dust of the earth. Grant that these ashes may be to us a sign of our mortality and penitence." I'd given ashes to a security guard, my thumb slipping over his flushed forehead in the sign of the cross, and to a woman in a white lab coat who moved her lips in silent prayer as I touched her face. "Far off yet here," we sang, "Far off yet here, the goal of all desire."

For the rest of that Wednesday, Will told me, more people than he expected kept popping in to his office on their breaks to receive ashes. "It was a relief, even for a lot of the docs, I think," he said. "All this effort goes into looking good, and working hard, and pretending you're in charge of life and death. What a relief to have a day when you're just another person with a smudge of dirt on your head."

Volunteers distributed ashes for a while from the back of the cafeteria, and then a young Episcopal priest who was one of Will's chaplain colleagues carried them to the beds of patients who'd asked to be included but were too sick to move. Their rooms would be cluttered with IV poles and monitors and uneaten trays of hospital food; sometimes a daughter or son would be keeping watch; often there was just an empty chair pushed into a corner. The priest would enter each room quietly, reaching into her pocket for the little jar. "Remember you're dust," she told the dying. "And to dust you shall return."

Some people meet God in a hospital bed. Some meet God in the wilderness, in the majesty of mountains, or under night skies; some feel God in the intimacy of trees shading a garden or in small, old villages. Paul makes regular retreats to a remote monastery in the desert, where the sand and silence scrub off the layers of cynicism that accumulate on his soul as he goes about the business of being a priest in San Francisco. Another friend I know spends time in North Carolina, where she can slow down to notice the redbush blooming, see birds that don't eat garbage, hear the wind in the trees at night. Martha can enter an almost trance-like state gardening in our back yard, weeding or deadheading or cutting back wisteria for hours. But for me, it's cities that make the presence of God most real.

In a way, St. Gregory's first taught me this. Certainly the rituals, the candles, the incense, the icons, the teaching and preaching, hymns and prayers I found inside that beautiful building opened my eyes. Certainly the torrents of Scripture I heard there—Psalms and parables, prophecies and Gospel stories—opened my ears. But it was the unedited, often uncomfortable experience of being jammed up bodily next to strangers at church, in liturgies; and at the food pantry, that cranked my heart open to the Word made flesh.

And that Word becomes even more vivid outside. On crowded urban streets, just as in the waiting room of the General, it's harder for me to avoid the knocking-together of lives that the Holy Spirit seems to relish so much. In the haphazard sprawl of a city, only the astronomically rich and walled-off can pretend that human ideas of order—like the geometric grid of county roads laid over the Great Plains, or the forced sameness and cleanliness of suburban shopping centers—are stable. The sheer unpredictability of city encounters makes it impossible to presume, as many churches do, that God's grace is sequential—measured out at regular intervals in baptism, confirmation, communion, marriage, burial—and will happen to everyone at the prescribed time, in the same way.

In a city, grace just falls all over the place. People march around in front of a supermarket carrying pictures of the saints, and I'm invited to kiss them. Strangers build altars in the courtyard of a housing project or denounce the *migra* on the plaza, and I'm invited to hold hands and pray with them. Jesus keeps dredging up odd fish in his net and dumping us all out, wriggling and shining, to reveal his Church.

I found Mr. Claws in the waiting room of the hospital pharmacy, clutching a blue trash bag with his few belongings in it and leaning slumped over against a wall. "Darling," he said hoarsely when he spotted me, and waved a crumpled piece of paper. "Got to get my medicine, but I don't have shoes." I looked down. He was wearing a pair of soiled white socks. "The lady said she'd look for some shoes for me," he said hazily, "but till she comes back I can't move."

I took the paper—it was a prescription for antibiotics, folded with a sheet of discharge instructions. "If you give me your ID," I said, "I can wait in line to drop off the prescription."

"Don't got ID," said Mr. Claws.

Over the next two hours, I waited in one line to register Mr. Claws without ID, another line to drop off his prescription, another line to pay for it, and another I got in by mistake; it would take, everyone assured me, two or three or five more hours before his medicine would actually be ready and I could stand in line again to pick it up. The pharmacy was crowded with angry, frustrated, sick, and crazy people trying to figure out where to go or arguing about who was first; a few lucky patients, like Mr. Claws, got turns sitting for a while in orange plastic chairs. Occasionally I asked someone to keep my place and went over to bring him water in a paper cup I'd begged from a friendly woman in the eligibility office. Mr. Claws drank thirstily but didn't talk; it seemed to take all his energy just to sit up.

I knew I'd have to leave soon, to go back to the church and gather our supplies for the Ash Wednesday service in the Mission. I looked around, at a loss, and caught the eye of the eligibility worker, a middle-aged black woman with deep red fingernails. "Social work never brought him those shoes, did they?" she asked. She sounded worn out. "Okay, I'm on till four," she said. "I'll keep an eye on him." I waved at her gratefully and bolted for my car.

I had no idea how much back-and-forth schlepping I was going to be doing on Ash Wednesday. Three steps forward, one step back: Mark and I joked this was the dance of the Christian life. But it felt endless.

I left the General, already feeling short of time, and drove back up the hill to St. Gregory's. The church doors were shut and locked, though there was a sign outside: *Ash Wednesday Services Tonight 7 p.m.* I felt bad for anyone who might stop by hoping to receive ashes during the day. There was nobody in the sanctuary: Mark and the parishioners were all at their jobs by now, Sanford

41

was gone until the evening service, and Paul was working in the cramped little office downstairs where he couldn't hear knocking on the church doors.

As with most congregations, we spent a large part of the budget on maintaining our space and making it beautiful, but it was vacant most of the week. Churches all over the country stay empty a great deal of the time: ministers in rural towns talk constantly about how their congregations are aging and shrinking, and their buildings go largely unused. "We're down to about, oh, fifteen people who show up once a week," a Midwestern pastor said to me once, exaggerating but honestly worried, "and their average age is eighty-five."

Yet when Mark and I had begun opening St. Gregory's for morning prayer, just half an hour each weekday, it was a revelation. When the doors were open, people would come in. This should have been obvious—I'd done it myself, after all—but it still surprised me. Kids heading to the high school up the block, workers in boots and overalls from the brewery across the street, commuters waiting for the bus, homeless guys offering to lend a hand with the food pantry, women with babies, coders on lunch break from one of the nearby software companies—it seemed they wanted something from the church. Sometimes it was a quick peek at the icons, or a bathroom, or directions. Sometimes it was breakfast, or to blurt out a confession, or to talk. The building was, it turned out, a sanctuary. Frequently strangers asked, shakily, if it was okay to just sit down for a minute. "I won't be long," they'd assure me. "I just want, I mean, is it okay if I pray here?"

One morning a wild, ancient Mexican bearded gnome-lady walked through the open doors just as I was about to blow out the candles and go home. I was pretty sure she lived near me in the Mission—I'd seen her around on the streets—but she had the angels' unnerving habit of appearing anywhere, unannounced, bearing cryptic messages. "*Ask* him," she half-shouted, waving her walking stick as she sailed through the doors pushing a little laundry cart. She was about four and a half feet tall, with a deeply creased face, huge buck teeth, white hair escaping from a woolen stocking cap, and an astonishing white beard. "Ask God what you need. My mother ask him. She make the children walk." The gnome-lady smiled. "Yes, she see that boy, say get up, boy! name of Jesus. He *get up*!"

She crossed herself and touched the icons and kept talking, nonstop, slowly and dramatically, in an impressionistic mix of English, Spanish, and gestures, telling Gospel stories. How she had seen the Virgin once when her mother was dying ("Bright, *very* bright") and how she had made a dumb child speak ("Ask God, touch the mouth, *ha*, name of Jesus, ha!").

I bent my head to her, as dutiful children in Latin America do when greeting their elders. "*La benedición*," I'd asked. Give me your blessing.

The gnome-lady reached up to touch me. Her beard looked soft, and her eyes were surprisingly clear. "God bless you and all the people come to this place and the church and bless always every one come in this door."

"Thank you, Doña..." I said, and she waved a hand perfunctorily. "You call me Nedi, it's okay, but my name is every name." She grabbed her shopping cart and headed back out. "*Ask* him," the gnome-lady repeated, and left the building.

I punched in my security code and entered St. Gregory's, propping a door open just in case someone showed up for ashes while I was here. The rotunda still smelled faintly of incense from the morning liturgy. I went into the church kitchen, making lists in my head as I packed a milk crate with the gear I'd need to bring to the Mission for our street service. Six little glass votive-candle holders, no, eight to be safe; fill them with ashes, cover tightly with plastic wrap—check. Six Ethiopian iron thuribles, one with a chain on the verge of breaking but should be okay with a bit of wire—check. A plastic baggie full of incense, lavender buds mixed with the super-smoky and fabulously named Benzoin Sumatra—check. Matches, of course, a lighter, of course, sooty blocks of charcoal—check. I wiped my hands on a dishcloth and stuck some paper towels in the crate, grateful that, according to Paul, since we weren't going to be celebrating Eucharist on the street, I was free to wear a black cassock. It was bad enough to have ashes and charcoal all over my hands, but if we were going to kneel on the street again, white would be a big mistake. Duct tape—check, you never know when you'll need duct tape. Pen, felt-tip marker, Book of Common Prayer.

I thought that should do it. I went to the vestry and pulled out one of the lighter-weight cotton cassocks, with a row of buttons from the neck to the hem. Check. I planned to put all the supplies in the trunk of my car and drive down the hill again to my house, where I could get something to eat and make a few calls. Then I'd go pick up Bertie Pearson, the young Episcopal priest who worked at Holy Innocents and St. John's and was going to lead the street service. Bertie lived just a few blocks from me; we'd use my car to go over to Holy Innocents and fetch a folding card table, then ferry everything to the plaza on Mission and 24th, where we'd start offering ashes at 4 p.m. I glanced at my watch. It was kind of weird, especially given our faith in God's incarnation, for me to text Paul instead of just walking down to the office and talking to him in the flesh, but now I was late. Or felt late, anyway, which I hated. *on my way to mission cu @7 xox,* I typed. Paul texted me back: *K.*

I had driven about halfway home along 24th Street when I said aloud, "God damn it," suddenly remembering what I'd forgotten to pack at St. Gregory's. I slammed on the brakes, a block past La Palma Mexicatessen, no doubt spilling charcoal out of the thuribles and getting the trunk of my dirty little Honda sedan even dirtier.

God damn it, I'd forgotten the Ash Wednesday posters. Bertie had made them so that people would know what we were doing. I was anxious enough about being out in public and having to explain our actions to strangers: the posters had seemed like a helpful crutch. Now it was going to take another half hour, at least, for me to make my way back through the crowded streets, drive all the way up the hill to church, find the posters, and come back down to the Mission again. I glared at a young bicyclist who was cutting ahead of me and tearing through the intersection. He didn't even have a helmet on, I noticed. Did he *want* to wind up at the emergency department in the General, getting a lecture about head trauma? Maybe I could catch Paul when I got to St. Gregory's and grab a quick lunch with him in Potrero Hill, or maybe there would still be time to stop at home for a sandwich, but this irritating detour made it seem unlikely. Real Christians were supposed to fast on Ash Wednesday, anyway. I sighed and turned around.

chapter four

Paradise is a garden, but heaven is a city. In the Revelation of John, the gates of the new Jerusalem are never shut. The holy city is built of gold, with walls of precious jewels and twelve gates made of pearls, and illuminated not by sun or moon or lamp but the pure glory of the Lord. The river of the water of life, "sparkling like crystal," flows down the middle of the street, watering the tree of life that yields fruit for food and leaves for the healing of the nations. There's no temple in the holy city, because God *is* the temple, and God dwells among his people, wiping their tears and making an end to death.

The Mission is located on a flat valley floor, protected by Bernal Hill to the south, Potrero Hill to the east, and a long rise to the west that climbs past Noe Valley all the way to Twin Peaks and the ridge separating the Bay side of San Francisco from the Pacific. A little river runs through the middle of the Mission, albeit underground, and trees line its bright streets. Even on days when ocean-front neighborhoods are completely socked in, fog tends to hang back at the ridge until late afternoon, when it pours over the divide and tumbles down 24th Street with gusts of wind. People can grow tomatoes in the Mission, and some even wear sunglasses. "Ah, the Mission," San Franciscans say knowingly. "Good weather over there."

The sun doesn't make the Mission particularly warmer than anywhere else in this chilly city, though, except during those few frighteningly still, piercingly blue-skied days in early autumn its residents refer to as "earthquake weather." But even on cool days, even in the rainy season, the streets are full of people. Despite tangles of bougainvillea everywhere, the Mission has none of the 1960s-California-garden-suburbs feel of the Western Sunset, for example, where topiary sentries guard neat, silent rows of stucco houses. Nor is it pretty in the way the twisting residential streets of Noe Valley or Potrero Hill are, with their flower-filled pocket parks and gold-trimmed Victorian homes perched on picturesque hills. The Mission is urban: unromantically smelly, unapolo-getically crowded, a place where families live above autobody shops, drunks sleep in playgrounds, and priests hear confessions in churches squeezed between butcher shops and bus stops.

The plaza at 24th and Mission is right in the middle of it all. A crossroads for the 14 and 48 MUNI buses, the 24th Street/Mission BART subway stop, and the lurching white van that shuttles between the subway and the San Francisco General Hospital, the plaza anchors the neighborhood's long commercial corridor. Commuters, shoppers, and residents roam through it constantly, but each part of the plaza is overseen by regulars who maintain their turf.

On the southeast corner of Mission and 24th, a McDonald's daubed with graffiti sells all-American industrial "tacos" to Mexican families. Underage Honduran dope dealers, pimply and pale, flank the restaurant's doors, watching for business and taking orders on their throwaway cell phones. Like the frightened Mixtec men peddling boxes of pesticide-laden oranges on nearby side streets, a lot of the boys are rumored to be indentured servants, working off debts to the gangs who brought them across the border. Too young to be sentenced to state prison, they serve as the child soldiers of drug wars until they grow up; by twenty-three or so, they return to the corner sporting tattoos—girls, teardrops, misspelled names—that mark the inevitable time they've done. Almost all of them wear crucifixes.

The northeast side holds a special attraction for the most hardcore Christian zealots, pacing up and down and haranguing passersby: "Lord, repent, Lord, burn, alleluia, amen, everlasting fire, repent..." Next to the shifty guys hustling bus transfers, they shout out prophecies through crappy little amps, accompanied by tambourines and clapping and the occasional psychotic preacher howling about hell so relentlessly that the transit cops finally make him go home.

To the northwest, a gaggle of old Nicaraguan men occupy overturned milk crates on the sidewalk and argue pointlessly about exile politics. A more or less Catholic religious-goods store, its windows clogged with rosaries and medallions and ugly plaster statues of Guadalupe and St. Joseph, is open only intermittently; its dusty back counter holds candles and powders that promise luck, money, revenge, love, protection from the evil eye. "*Yo Puedo Y Tu No*" reads one little envelope of powder, printed with the image of a grinning strongman; another features a haughty woman in 1940s heels boasting "I Dominate My Man." Some junkies linger nearby at the doors of a Chinese restaurant where tired workers ladle greasy noodles into take-out containers; up the street, cool black girls with iPods and nose rings climb the stairs to a *capoeira* studio.

The southwest side of the plaza, near the bus stop, is claimed by a band of *salseros*, who use it as their performance space and social club on weekends, enticing even the tough butch girls with baggy pants to pause when the singer, a stocky Puerto Rican guy in his seventies, lets his tenor slide over the stutter of claves in "Cuando Te Vea." The *congero* hunches over his drums impassively, but lifts his head and calls out praise to the *orixas* as Yoruba chants break out from deep inside the familiar rhythms, and ancient spirits seem to hover over the sidewalk.

Oblivious, a few Jehovah's Witnesses usually stand across from the musicians: plain middle-aged women in glasses and long skirts, silently holding up copies of the Spanish-language *Watchtower* that nobody ever takes. Next to them, where the BART escalator pours out commuters, the food vendors park their carts: men grilling hot dogs with bacon, guys selling hot ears of corn drenched in mayonnaise and salty cheese, women with coolers full of homemade tamales wrapped in banana leaves, and the ubiquitous *paleteros* ringing their bells as they peddle Popsicles and luridly colored blooms of cotton candy.

Long before I lived in the neighborhood, I'd seen that plaza. When I was twenty-five and facing hot summer months in a steamy New York City kitchen, I quit my job as a prep cook and hitched a ride with two co-workers heading to the West Coast. We piled the car with sleeping bags and drove across America, stopping only for gas and pie.

The streets were foggy and mysterious when we arrived, late one night, and made our way up creaking outdoor stairs to a third-floor flat in the Mission. I'd sent a letter to Nina, a wild and slightly crazy Puerto Rican girl I knew from New York, who lived with a quiet but much crazier boyfriend from East Texas. They had a mattress on the floor and an aluminum pot of hot espresso waiting for us; over the next weeks, they'd show me around what they called, simply, "the city."

To a New Yorker this "city" was almost laughably bucolic: Nina and Dave spent whole afternoons lounging on the grass under actual palm trees in Dolores Park, eating actual mangoes and smoking dope, until actual stars filled the night sky and the air was thick with the sharp licorice scent of wild fennel. There were no express trains, no newsstands, and very few cabs. Most of the painted wooden houses in the Mission were just three stories tall, and Nina seemed to know all the shopkeepers in the little corner stores dotting the neighborhood. "Doreen!" she'd greet someone in a dusty bakery, flashing her brilliant hustler smile. "Look! Here's my girlfriend from back East, can you give us two of those beautiful almond buns and I'll pay you tomorrow?"

The city's left-wing culture, though, "the movement," was vibrant and influential. Nowhere was it more vital than in the Mission, where Latino activists worked to transform disparate neighbors into a community. There were Chicano muralists and white Vietnam veterans; American Indian Movement activists and Gay Liberation hell-raisers; militant trade unionists and IRA gunrunners; a dozen fiercely warring ultra-militant socialist parties, each with maybe two dozen members; Black Panthers; women in combat boots who raised money for the Cuban revolution and men in combat boots who wore dresses. There were collectives and communes and "movement houses," and you could buy all your groceries from uber-crunchy food co-ops run by Chicana feminists and white welfare moms.

What anyone sees at twenty-five is limited. Entire chunks of the Mission—the Irish Mission of working-class bars, the proudly Polish Mission with its "Literary and Dramatic Circle" of artistic exiles, the Mexican-American Mission of home-owning families whose only remotely political activity was voting the straight Democratic ticket—remained invisible to me. And it would be decades before I noticed the wildly varied spiritual life and religious faith of the Mission.

Compared to other American cities, San Francisco seems strikingly secular. In 2010, according to the Association of Religious Data Archives, just over a third of San Francisco's residents (as compared to seventy percent of Americans) went to religious services or professed any religious faith; in a national survey in 2013, Gallup ranked the San Francisco Bay Area as among the five "least religious" metro regions in the country. Richard Florida, an editor with *The Atlantic Cities*, suggests that it isn't about location per se: he argues that Gallup's data simply show a correlation between religiosity and "income, education, and occupation." A decline in working-class jobs, an increase in "knowledge, professional and creative" workers, and a rise in income will lower the number of residents who say they are "very religious" and also attend religious services. In some cities, a steady influx of poor immigrants keeps Catholic and Pentecostal churches full; but everywhere neighborhoods are gentrifying and younger residents dominate, churches are losing members. In other words, poor people believe in God; working-class people mostly believe in God; wealthier, more educated and "modern" people don't bother.

But statistics can't tell the whole story. Because even San Francisco—this rich, secular, young, high-tech city— is teeming with faith, both inside churches and outside. It's particularly noticeable in the Mission. The oldest building in San Francisco is in the Mission, the first settled area of the city, and it's a church. In early 1776, Spanish explorers came up the peninsula scouting for new settlement sites; on June 29 of that year, two Spanish priests established the Mission San Francisco de Asis in a temporary chapel, near what they named the Lake of our Mother of Sorrows, Dolores. With the name of God on their lips, the Spaniards began to enslave and forcibly convert the Ohlone Indians they found there, and the Church was in business.

Today, within walking distance of the original Mission Dolores, there are six thriving Catholic parishes and their attached schools; a crimson, steepled 1880s Lutheran church converted at vast expense into the Hua Zang Si Buddhist temple and monastery; a large and shabby Kingdom Hall of the Jehovah's Witnesses; two Spanish-speaking Southern Baptist congregations; the sweet, wood-shingled Episcopal Church of the Holy Innocents; a Lutheran church where old ladies sing in German; a pretty, freshly painted Iglesia Adventista del 7 Dia, wedged between a tax-prep office and a nail salon; two swaybacked Presbyterian churches (one Korean and one Salvadoran); a Salvation Army outpost; the Episcopal Church of St. John the Evangelist; the mostly Nicaraguan congregation of Santa Maria y Santa Marta Lutheran; a few home congregations of Candomblé, Santería, and Voudou worshippers; two home churches of emergent-evangelical white Jesus freaks; a gay Reform synagogue, where a Mennonite congregation also meets on Sundays; a convent of the Sisters of Charity; a Franciscan house; several Assemblies of God; a huge fenced nondenominational fortress with the word "Christian" blazing in blue neon letters from its impenetrable ramparts; at least ten Pentecostal storefront churches, including the "Lyre of the Valley," the "Pillar and Ground of Truth," and the "Rock of Salvation," whose members cook and sell barbecue on the sidewalk after services; the interfaith chapel at the San Francisco General Hospital; and a dazzling assortment of botánicas, meditation centers, chapels, bookstores, and shrines dedicated to popular belief.

Church equals church buildings, right? So if you want to find God, any one of these would seem like a good place to start. As I found out when I first crossed St. Gregory's threshold, and as Mark and I discovered when we started doing morning prayer, an open church door is an invitation all kinds of people find hard to resist. In a lonely and commercial world, sanctuaries still matter: both the shabby little rooms of Lyre of the Valley and the spacious nave of Mission Dolores continue to speak to the deep desire for a set-apart place to rest and pray. Once I became part of a congregation, I could understand the profound meaning church buildings everywhere carry for their communities, as well as for strangers. Inside the wooden ribs of St. Gregory's, I felt held as safely as the infant Jesus in his mother's arms.

But once my eyes were opened, and my attention tuned, it became clear how that isn't the whole story. It's not just inside church buildings that you can find God: in the holy city, God *is* the temple and dwells among his people. The people cross themselves before lunch in a break room or a school, process down the street carrying pictures of the Virgin Mary, pray in parks, light candles on their stoops to honor the dead, gather with crosses to sing hymns and protest immigration laws. Plenty of poor people in San Francisco, like the homeless guys who build shrines in their encampment under the bridge, converse freely and intimately with God in public. And so do some rich, ostensibly modern people: they hold Bible study in the conference room of a downtown investment bank or send prayers via Twitter to their co-workers at a tech company. The city might be far less religious than most if measured by the number of people who attend churches, but in its streets it's the city of God.

San Francisco boasts a historic identity as a mixed-up, "wide-open" port, populated by sailors, adventurers, immigrants, gamblers, gold-diggers, loose women, beatniks, hippies, activists, and queers. But it also has roots as a deeply Catholic town, and the collective religious vibe of the city owes a lot to the complicated expressions of Roman Catholicism found here.

Though its leadership fights to keep the doctrine pure, the faith is constantly contaminated, syncretized, revered, and tinkered with by its adherents—and by outsiders like me, who it continues to influence. It's sentimental and businesslike, the faith of superstitious peasants and of brainy postmodern Jesuits. It's undergirded a great deal of radical immigrant and labor activism for generations, but it's also been a reactionary force wielding money and power in support of political bosses.

And long after respectable Protestant denominations retreated inside, emerging from their church buildings only for graveside services—leaving just Holy Rollers, Mormons, and unaffiliated madwomen to evangelize alfresco—Catholics kept marching out into the streets of San Francisco for processions, festivals, blessings, and liturgies at the slightest excuse. In the Mission, they display statues of saints at outdoor altars bedecked with marigolds for the Day of the Dead, along with aluminum trays of home-cooked desserts to feed the living and the dead. They lay candles and flowers and empty rum bottles at the bases of lampposts, beneath pictures of murder victims and announcements of upcoming funeral Masses. They carry banners of the Virgin of Guadalupe in union marches, demonstrations, and the annual procession to Dolores Park for the "Aztec Quinceañera," a girls' rite of passage where bare-torsoed men in feather headdresses chant prayers to the four directions.

The Mission's public panorama of faith is unavoidable. My whole neighborhood is God's city. How did I manage to not pay attention for so long, when God is sending out signs as unsubtly as a Popsicle vendor ringing the bells on his pushcart and screeching *paleeetas* to announce his presence?

chapter five

A s I doubled back along 24th Street to fetch the Ash
Wednesday posters from St. Gregory's, I tried to
breathe deeply. It was here on these streets, after all, where
we'd be offering ashes in just a few hours. Maybe being
forced to retrace the route now was a good thing: it would
make me slow down. Every four-way stop sign was an opportunity to observe, to consider my neighbors, maybe
even to pray in preparation for the afternoon's outdoor
liturgy. "*Now is the acceptable time*," I hummed to myself,
"*now is the hour of repentance...*"

I passed the gigantic portrait of the Virgin of
Guadalupe on the wall of La Palma Mexicatessen. Across
the street, at St. Peter's Catholic Church, with its murals
of saints and martyrs, the doors were open for Ash
Wednesday services. I stopped halfway through the in-

tersection to let a guy steer his pushcart, wobbly with great slabs of *chicarrones* and bottles of hot sauce, up the curb. A woman sidestepped him, crossing herself reflexively as she passed the church, and waved thanks to me as I waited at the wheel, impatiently.

What was it that felt so compelling about observing Ash Wednesday outside, especially given the Gospel reading appointed for the day? In it, Jesus lectures show-offs like me: "Whenever you pray, do not be like the hypocrites, for they love to stand and pray in the synagogues and at the street corners, so that they may be seen by others."

I didn't altogether love to be seen by others: frequently I felt embarrassed and self-conscious, as in those classic nightmares about speaking in public wearing only underpants.

"Oh, my God, Sara," my wife groaned the first time I told her where I was planning to be on Ash Wednesday. "Are you really going out to the plaza in, like, full church drag?"

As difficult as it had sometimes been for Martha when I started attending services on Sundays, I knew this was a whole other step. San Francisco's mongrel religious culture had finally caught up with me. "Yeah," I said. "Well, you know, just a few of us, just a little service. Sort of. Ashes. I mean—look, what can I say, I've gone over the edge."

I tried to sound casual, but the line between respectable churchgoer and lunatic evangelist had been rapidly eroding. Even Roman Catholics didn't offer ashes in the plaza. And I hadn't told Martha we were planning to kneel on the sidewalk in cassocks and pray.

So why work so hard to hold a church service outside of church, especially when it was potentially humiliating? Was this just a break in routine for bored liturgists, a flirtation with the exotic? Were we engaging in a kind of extreme religious sport? Following a trendy fad? Making a statement to show how innovative and daring we could be?

Paul helped me think through what it would mean to carry ashes outside. Ash Wednesday, he explained, "is one of those weird commemorations" that doesn't correspond to any specific event in the life of Jesus, or of any saint. "That's why," he said, "in the proper liturgy for the day, it's the Church that issues the call to observe a holy Lent, rather than God herself. Ash Wednesday is something the *Church* does—which makes it easy to keep it inside the walls of the temple."

Paul didn't like to lead street liturgies himself—he found the experience chaotic and "too distracting." Yet he supported me fully in taking ashes to the streets, believing it was important not to privilege buildings over bodies in worship. The liturgies he wrote were about connecting people physically, as well as through words and music. The reason he asked congregants at St. Gregory's to impose ashes on one another was so they could experience, in their own flesh, the truth of their shared mortality. So Paul understood why I hoped that outside the temple, without any beautiful icons or ritual silences to cushion it, the truth might be felt—and shared—even more immediately.

I wondered if this was what Vera, a hospice social worker from Texas who was new to St. Gregory's, also sought. In her early thirties, with cropped blond hair, Vera seemed a bit reserved at first, hanging back at the edges of worship. But when I announced the schedule of Ash Wednesday services, Vera immediately asked to help with the one in the streets of the Mission. We talked: She'd been very involved in lay leadership at her church in Texas, but hinted she'd left after a personal tragedy. "I just had some really distorted ideas about what I can expect from God," Vera said carefully, "and so I'm adjusting how I relate to church."

But she said she was drawn to liturgy practiced outside

church walls. "When you receive ashes in a church," Vera said, "you have to work a little to connect it to the world, to suffering and loss and absence. Out on the street, there are still plenty of distractions, but the scars are going to be visible, everyone's life and death is mixed up. You're not going to get the ashes and pretend it's not true."

Worship outside of church buildings is the unexceptional historical and contemporary norm for Christianity, and almost all other religions. The newer and less traditional practice is formal liturgy held inside a place used once a week for purely religious purposes, with people sitting in orderly rows, facing the same direction, and reading aloud in unison.

Worship happens outside all the time. During Holy Week in Spain, it happens when crowds of all ages throng the streets of their cities in processions, and ordinary housewives standing on the corner suddenly burst forth with keening, Arabic-inflected *saetas,* improvised songs of devotion to Mary and Jesus that sound as if their hearts are being pulled from their chests.

It happens in places like the Buddhist temple I visited in Myanmar, an ancient open-air complex with twelfth-century statues wreathed in blinking Christmas lights, where a saffron-robed monk chanted scriptures as three boys on the mat next to him played Monopoly, and women came and went selling snacks, occasionally dropping to kneel and pray on soft, smooth teak platforms.

It happens in homes. "I don't try to convince Cris or anyone else to come to church," Mark explained to me once. "But I can make God's presence more real to other people. I bring God closer to us when I love Cris: help her heal after surgeries, make a place for her to do what she wants to do in the world. The relationship is my mission field, my vocation."

Worship happens during tent revivals and televangelism, river baptisms and the blessing of fishing fleets, picnics in graveyards or prayers on Facebook. It's hard to contain the human thirst for worship in boundaried religious rituals run by designated religious professionals taking place in set-apart religious buildings; God so seldom means just one thing to any individual, much less the same one thing at a time to a whole group.

And so worship spills out every place God meets people: in Jewish prayers at a family table, at Hindu roadside shrines, among Italian-American Catholics lugging statues of Mary through their suburban neighborhoods, and Muslims praying at noon on a little scrap of carpet set down beside a tractor trailer in some light-industrial junkyard. It happens in bedrooms, in hospital waiting rooms, in jails, in cars; not to mention on the dusty roads in the polluted outskirts of town, where Jesus walked and prayed and healed.

It just requires paying attention. As deacons in the Orthodox Church boom out, instructing the flock before reading Scripture aloud: *Wisdom: attend!*

I was walking one day, distractedly, down 24th Street on my way to the bank. "Look!" I heard a voice command. It was that old bearded Mexican gnome-lady, appearing out of nowhere in front of me. She stopped, shaking her head, and reached out a hand. "*Look,*" she said to me again forcefully, and uncurled her fingers from around a small, hard, yellow lemon. "For you," she said. "Take it. God bless."

God's blessing is everywhere. And so paying attention outside of church buildings—as well as paying attention inside church buildings—becomes a way to see more of God from different angles, uncovering more meanings. Whether in the midst of a literal city, or in the suburbs, or on a lonely mountainside, worship outside of church buildings allows a glimpse of the world, the whole world, transformed.

I looked at my watch. Where had the morning gone?

chapter six

It was around two by the time I made it back to St. Gregory's, picked up the posters, and arrived home in the Mission again. I'd stopped by my office and gotten stuck there for longer than I planned, trading back-and-forth calls with a social worker in San Mateo County who'd unaccountably taken a real interest in tracking down Mr. Claws.

"That sounds terrible," he said when I phoned the first time. "Listen, if you can find the address he gave at the General, I'll just drive over there myself and knock on his door. I can make sure he's okay."

But when he called me back the social worker was deflated. "There's no apartment building at that address," he said, bemused. "I just found an empty lot. It's not a real place."

I recalled how Mr. Claws always insisted he didn't have a phone, and how Mark had never been able to convince him to accept a ride "home" or to "work" after morning prayer. Why was he so intent on hiding from us? Briefly, I considered going back to the General and hunting for Mr. Claws in the pharmacy, or on the benches outside where dazed patients often sat, released from the emergency department into homelessness, clutching papers for return appointments they'd never keep. But the day was running away from me; I made a mental note to call Will at the chaplaincy office and ask him to check around the General for Mr. Claws. I remembered the old man saying, "I was *worried* about you," and hoped to return the favor.

"Lord have mercy," I said to the social worker. "Thank you so much; let's check in tomorrow."

I found a parking space in front of the elementary school near my house and got out of the car with a long black cassock draped over one arm. It was still before the end of the school day, so only a small pile of trash swirled around my feet. By three in the afternoon, when hungry kids poured out to the waiting pushcart vendors, the sidewalk would be covered in debauched heaps of ice cream wrappers, discarded hot-chips packets, and math worksheets. I kicked away a soft drink cup irritably, crossed the street, and climbed up the stairs to my home.

Maybe it was because of the back and forth all day, and my anxiety about being late, or maybe just because of the approaching street liturgy, but I badly needed to eat some solid food and settle down. I pushed the iron gate to our porch open, unlocked the door, and laid my cassock on the bench, under a shelf that held a plastic Virgin of Guadalupe figurine Paul had given me and a little bouquet of jasmine blossoms. There were always fresh flowers in our house. Martha and I spent a ridiculous amount of time in the backyard, cooing over our flowers and fruit trees and shrubs and trying to hack back the vines—jasmine, honeysuckle, trumpet vine, and wisteria—before they completely swallowed everything. I picked off a browned petal from the bouquet, reflexively, dropped my keys on the shelf, and walked into the sunny kitchen.

There was only about an hour and a half left to check some e-mail, have a sandwich, and calm my nerves before I had to fetch Bertie and start giving ashes on the plaza. Then we'd finally be *doing* it, instead of anticipating it, which I hoped would be easier. I opened the door to the refrigerator. Swiss chard, milk, yogurt, seltzer, butter, *nam pla* fish sauce, some dried-up cheddar, a jar of red plum jam. "No fasting," Paul had warned me the year before. "Not if you're going to be working on Ash Wednesday. It's tacky to pass out in front of everyone." Amen, I thought. Oh, there were some tortillas and half a loaf of bread that didn't look too stale. Maybe grilled cheese?

The first time I saw the big wooden house in the Mission District it was summer, and there were tomatoes and zinnias poking their heads through the tall weeds in its overgrown backyard. I had a growing four-year-old and a shrinking relationship with her father, no job, and no idea whether San Francisco was going to be anything more than a temporary sojourn before the life I assumed was my real one would resume, in New York or maybe Managua.

The bright blue house was, people said, a movement house: it had been passed along through a loosely knit transnational network of left-wing activists. It would turn out that I knew, through connections, each person who'd owned it since 1970.

Gilberto Arriaza, the friend of a friend from Central

America, had bought the house with his wife Naomi after they'd left Guatemala during the war. Now they wanted to rent it out, possibly sell it: they had two kids and a muscular boxer dog, and their daughter was heading for middle school. "It's too dangerous right now in the Mission," said Gilberto, who had survived an epoch of death squads and scorched-earth campaigns by the Guatemalan army. He was a trim, dark-haired activist with glasses, an advocate for bilingual education. "Too much gang stuff. I want my kids to be able to, you know, go outside by themselves."

That sounded reasonable. But our child was hardly at risk for falling under the influence of blunt-smoking, lipstick-wearing, dope-peddling teenage hoodlums; Katie was years away from wandering anywhere but the living room by herself. And the Mission felt reassuringly familiar to me—far more comfortable than the ostensibly safer but virtually empty residential streets of Potrero Hill, the San Francisco neighborhood where we'd first landed. Everything there had been mannerly and contained and quiet; despite a shining view of the great Bay, our little apartment felt cut off and isolated. I was adrift in America and feared I could go for weeks without encountering or speaking to another person.

The Mission seemed like coming home. There were always people thronging the streets: washing their trucks, herding their children into a playground, lugging massive sacks of laundry to the corner. They actually talked with each other. I'd stop by a beat-up van full of watermelons on Folsom Street, and a man in a cowboy hat would thump a few before choosing the perfect melon and handing it over with a poker-faced promise. "*Garantizada por vida*," he'd say. "Guaranteed for life." The Mission smelled like my barrio in Managua and sounded like my old street in New York: it would be heaven to be back living in a real city.

I wondered if Gilberto's house was the answer to my prayers. Built in 1917, it still boasted built-in cabinets, thick glass French doors in the dining room, and a wide Edwardian staircase that led upstairs to three bedrooms. The plumbing and electricity didn't seem as if they'd ever been updated, but the place had clearly been worked over, to its distress, by many hapless hippie carpenters in the early 1970s. The original redwood planks had been painted over and the ceilings "textured"; the kitchen was tricked out with laminated modular cabinets and yellow bubble glass; dark splintery lathing was tacked in creative diagonal stripes all over the walls; the stairs were covered in stained green carpet and the bathroom featured more dark lathing, with a dying plant hung in a macramé planter. The basement, which Gilberto said vaguely had been used as some kind of "liberation school" for some kind of refugees from some indeterminate Latin American location, was low-ceilinged and dank. It had a grim little toilet, a few long, wide shelves that looked suspiciously like bunks, and cubbies painted with names: *Gustabo. Eduardo.* Upstairs, the bedrooms were lit by big, beautiful windows: one looked out toward the bright murals of the bustling public elementary school Katie could eventually attend. From the others you could see a neighbor's towering avocado tree, an ugly bank building over on Mission Street, and, far away, a radio tower blinking out messages from the top of Twin Peaks.

The green stucco house next door was split into two flats; Thad Povey, a cheerful young white guy, was working in his immaculately organized garage and waved as we went up the stairs. "He and Janet live downstairs," said Gilberto. "Thad can lend you any tool you need."

Gilberto completed the tour by introducing me to Don Miguel, a stooped older Mexican man in a baseball cap who, he said, had raised seven children in the pink-shingled single-family house on the other side. Don

Miguel seemed very shy, but he nodded, shook my hand, and mumbled *bienvenida* nonetheless.

I considered what I'd seen. The house had exactly one electrical outlet in each of its bedrooms, and a bathtub full of fish under a lemon tree in its enormous, scruffy backyard, and even as Gilberto had explained the dicey plumbing, which featured a garden hose draining the kitchen sink, I'd known, in under five minutes, that this was going to be my home, and that I would do whatever it took to make sure I could live there for the rest of my life.

To call a place a movement house begs the question of what anyone means by a movement. What Gilberto and others in the Mission meant by it was somewhat reminiscent of what I'd seen in the old days visiting Nina and Dave, but even more complex. For decades, progrowth forces in San Francisco—developers, banks, and their political representatives—had tried to make inroads into the Mission and were beaten back by a Latino-led coalition of neighbors defending their homes and cultures. The fight was still on. I didn't know any church people then—

though churches were at the forefront of a great deal of grassroots organizing, especially among immigrants—but I was amazed by the Mission's landscape of secular activists. They organized tenants and teachers, fought predatory landlords and lenders; they planted community gardens, marched against the violence of cops and gangs alike, won legal rights for immigrants, and forced the city to keep their neighborhood schools and health clinics open.

I wasn't sure how I'd fit in to this movement. My old position of reporter—inside enough to be close to whatever was happening, but outside enough to not be responsible—had been familiar and comfortable. Committing myself, heart and soul, to collective action with any particular place and people felt risky. How would I know what was the right place, the right people? Couldn't I just move in, try to pay attention, and be a good neighbor?

I wasn't a joiner. But I wanted something bigger than myself. I nursed a hope that the movement, with all its flaws, could bring me together with others to build community. That solidarity among all the different parts making up the whole would be lasting, even if we argued. And that shared values, if not shared experience, could unite me with others—like Gilberto or Mark or the watermelon guy—as I made my home alongside others in this new city.

This is, of course, a profoundly religious hope. It is the hope of the Christian Church—which is a movement, as well as an institution— over the centuries since its birth. But I didn't know enough to connect the dots between the deep longing to be part of a mystical body and the desires for community expressed in neighborhood political meetings. It would be a long time before I heard St. Paul's words to the quarrelsome little churches he visited and could relate his plea for unity to the secular movement. "There are varieties of gifts," the apostle admonished his fractious sisters and brothers, not entirely gently, "but the same Spirit... To each is given the manifestation of the Spirit, for the common good."

I would discover that hope for the Church, like hope for a movement, can flourish right alongside despair over our sins. In a meeting to plan Ash Wednesday services in the street, an enthusiastic deacon cornered me. "It's so cool," he said, "that we're doing this for the people!" I nodded, but hearing the phrase that was so omnipresent in my political life filled me with a bleak rage. It was hard to trust that anyone who comfortably invoked "the people" had the slightest clue about how annoying real people were—or how intelligent and resourceful. The presumption that the deacon or I were doing anything "for" this mythical people set my teeth on edge.

I hated the thought that being a Christian meant making the same kind of mistakes I'd made as a secular activist all over again. I remembered a handsome young man from one of El Salvador's revolutionary parties who'd bring leaflets to a little tailor shop in the capital and scold the woman who ran it—someone who risked her life to keep track of the disappeared—for not being "militant" enough. I remembered my own professional conviction that I could help protect a Filipino peasant we interviewed in the jungles of Luzon who was afraid of government soldiers—though if I'd listened more closely it would have come clear his family was in fact being menaced by the guerrillas who were my friends.

In movements, we often want to be right in our assumptions more than we want to receive the truth from others. It's so much easier to develop schematic theories about the behavior of classes than to spend years in the grind of listening to real human beings and finding out all the complicated things they really want. It's so much easier to offer analysis of the correct path than to see where people are already going themselves.

And the Church does the same thing. Thanks to a third-world critique of mission work in the colonial and postcolonial eras, there's some consciousness about the problem of English and American Christians deciding that other cultures' theologies are deficient or absent. But a lot of Christians, liberals as well as conservatives, still easily assume that sex workers, punk rockers, or young parents strolling along 24th Street don't have their own revelations and theologies: they just need to get with the program and come to know God the right way—ours. We're willing to translate a bit, to dress Jesus up with contemporary images or what we imagine to be culturally appropriate kinds of music, but basically we know the answers. God, the real God, is already revealed inside my own church building, or inside my denomination, and if I'm generous enough, I can offer the good news to unfortunates waiting for it on street corners.

But Christians—whether heading outdoors in cassocks on Ash Wednesday, or hollering "Repent!" on the plaza at rush hour through their amps—are hardly "bringing Church to the streets." We're simply witnessing to the reality that Church—not the buildings or tax-exempt legal entities, but the complex, contradictory body of Christ—is already there. "The people" are God's people. They are already living in the holy city of God. They're out in the streets encountering Jesus, Mary, saints, demons, angels, themselves, and one other—sometimes a lot more intensely than is comfortable. They're out there praying, sinning, repenting, blessing, being baptized into the muddy river of new life. They're not waiting for missionaries with the correct theology to save them. *God* is saving them, and, God willing, will save me, too, from my own pretensions, and keep on forging us into members of one body, for the common good.

Over the two decades since I moved into Gilberto's house, the common good took quite a beating in America. Christians murdered one another in the name of life, one antiabortion activist even shooting a doctor in church on a Sunday morning as he was greeting worshippers. Leftists fought one another in the name of the masses: stealing money, taking each other to court, screaming at their comrades, and threatening defectors. Believers and potential believers left churches and political movements in droves, as horrific, long-hidden stories of sexual abuse, lies, and violence by leaders came to light. The churches suffered, to be sure, as did the movements, but the fall was made harder because any honest person could see how much of it was caused by the movements' and the churches' own pride, dishonest self-interest, and, as Jesus would say, sadly, "hardness of heart."

In 2010, a group of young cartographers and reporters made a book of maps about the Mission, focusing on the collapse of the common good in the neighborhood. There was a map that correlated upscale stores selling cute cupcakes with blocks controlled by Sureño and Norteño gangs; there was a series of maps showing the decline—precipitous in some sections, including on my own block—of Latino residents; there were maps indicating the shrinking availability of any rental housing. There was a map of trees, including the surprising oranges that winked from so many backyards, and a map of "spiritual places," though it excluded the many Pentecostal and nondenominational churches. But my hopeful picture of the Mission as a place where ordinary people could seek and find the common good together—eating fruit, praying, hanging out—was disappearing. The maps were beautiful and the facts were hard.

It's not that earthly cities ever remain static: new immigrants displace older ones, family-run stores that anchor a neighborhood go out of business, earthquakes and floods tear up natural boundaries, and powerbrokers gerrymander new political lines to suit their own purposes. But the changes in the Mission were accelerating. The old dive bar where Nina and Dave had taken me was still doing a brisk business before noon. But now there were also restaurants with extensive wine lists, artisanal ice cream stores, and carefully curated clothing shops where hand-made sweaters cost a couple hundred bucks. As I flipped through the book of maps, I tried to comfort myself by remembering a previous boom time, when Latino activists in the Mission rallied against gentrification, and angry punk kids vandalized "yuppie" cars, convinced that the neighborhood was on the brink of utter destruction. That boom went bust and the software start-ups moved out, and the falling-down ghetto shoe store on the corner of 23rd was finally replaced by a different falling-down ghetto shoe store. Maybe things would be okay. There were still plenty of dollar stores in the Mission, I reassured myself, and Laundromats, and Casa Guadalupe still sold limes for ten cents each and would let you pay later if you forgot your wallet.

By 2012, though, the gentrification of San Francisco

had reached a new level, changing the face of even the historically resistant Mission. Pushed by a coalition of developers, the city gained 40,000 high-tech workers in just under two years, an influx that drove rents skyward and sparked a furious wave of luxury-apartment construction. There were fewer union members and more bankers living in San Francisco, fewer churchgoers and more fancy-restaurant-goers, fewer beds in the county hospital and more prisoners in the county jail. A Mission community organization had successfully pressured the city to finally clear out an empty corner lot full of toxic waste near our house: it was a garden and playground now, optimistically called Niños Unidos, constantly crammed with happily yelling toddlers. But where were those kids' parents supposed to work, if any more of the small businesses that used to surround the playground went under? Maybe there'd be a few jobs for dishwashers at expensive restaurants like the offensively named "Local's Corner," which charged three dollars for bread and butter. Maybe some rich people would hire nannies to take their children to Niños Unidos. But local hardware stores, paint stores, stationery stores, and fabric stores kept closing. Cris and other dogged legal activists fought hard to keep elderly tenants from being evicted, but when small landlords sold their rickety buildings to be demolished and quickly replaced by lofts renting for $3,000 a month, where were regular people supposed to live? What kind of movement, what kind of faith, could possibly turn this all around? I was part of the changes sweeping through the Mission, as a white lady who had bought a big house from a Guatemalan couple for an unimaginably small sum back in the day. Now my own daughter couldn't afford to live here. I didn't know what to do, or what repentance, real change, for all of us might look like.

But it was Ash Wednesday, and I needed lunch. I slapped some chunks of cheddar into a stale tortilla; the food wasn't satisfying. I made a cup of coffee, then poured it out. Too wired to really rest, and too tired to accomplish anything, I dithered at my desk a bit, answering e-mails, then poked around the backyard. I knew it was time to go, but realized how anxious I felt about leaving my house. I was going to have to encounter my neighbors when I went outside.

There's no way to be a Christian at home by yourself. I pulled on the black cassock over my clothes, looking in a mirror to button up the long row of buttons and adjust the sleeves, wondering if I'd be too cold, or hot, and what people who had to wear vestments every day did with their wallets and keys. I grabbed another roll of paper towels, just in case. I fingered the Virgin of Guadalupe medallion around my neck, saying a little prayer that it wouldn't rain. And that I wouldn't trip on the hem of the cassock. And that—oh, Lord have mercy. Let it be real.

chapter seven

Vecino: neighbor. It was a common form of address in the Mission, somewhere between the church's "brother" or "sister" and the movement's "comrade." It was at the very heart of Jewish and Christian teaching: *love God; love your neighbor*. And it was my own vocational aspiration: ever since settling here, awkward as I might feel, I yearned to be part of the neighborhood, to be grounded by it, to become a ground for others.

One of Don Miguel's grown children next door, Linda, sometimes shared her vision of neighborliness. Leaning over the railing of her messy deck, twisting her long black ponytail, she'd free-associate with me about the old days. "Yeah, we used to go all the way down to the corner through everyone's backyard," she reminisced, "climbing over fences, like we lived in the country." In a sense, the Mission of her childhood, despite its grand movie theaters and crowded buses, *was* the country: a place where grandmothers killed chickens and cut *nopal* paddles in their gardens for dinner; a place where too many people knew all your family's business.

That much hadn't changed. Now it was mostly white hipsters who raised chickens and planted vegetables in their backyards, but the friendly small-town feel of much of the Mission remained—at least in the romantic narrative Linda and I favored. "Sure, it was really dangerous for a while," she agreed as we discussed the years when I'd first moved here. "But now, look, there's a lot of people on the block again, not just drug people and gangs, but families."

"I know," I said, self-satisfied, "isn't it *great* to know your neighbors?"

But in truth the "drug people" had never gone away, any more than the gangs that had worried Gilberto. The new upper-middle-class families were as screwed up and dysfunctional as the old working-class families. And I had spent all those years trying *not* to know my neighbors— or at least not to know them well enough to really love them.

I hadn't even learned the last name of Ricardo, for ex-

ample, the young activist from our block who kept inviting me to meetings, and I was predisposed to like him. He
walked around the neighborhood with petitions about
jobs and gentrification, urged everyone to register to vote,
and maintained an enthusiasm for "the community" that
gave me a surge of nostalgic pleasure. Behold, I thought:
another generation still believes in the movement. Ricardo was a little goofy, he wasn't the world's greatest
organizer, but he was persistent and generous. I loved the
way he and his girlfriend threw a street party for all their
vecinos in the summer, and at Christmas painstakingly
strung lights on the concrete patio in front of their apartment house to spell out "HAPPY HOLIDAYS."

Other neighbors, though, actively annoyed me, as
when Geraldo, a skinny, falling-down drunk who lived a
few doors down, decided to embark on a wave of community beautification projects. "To give back," he slurred.
"I just wanna give back to the block." Late at night, he'd
rip out handfuls of weeds from the wells around the street
trees and scratch shallow furrows in the dry, hard-packed,
dog-pee-enhanced dirt. Then he'd lay down some random
plants—nobody wanted to know where he'd procured
them—and pile gravel over the roots. Voilà: gardens. In
the well in front of our house, Geraldo hadn't been able to

dig a hole deep enough for his droopy jade plant to stand up, so he'd tied it to the tree with some electrical wire. Then he'd stuck in three yellow onions, which he apparently hoped would turn into onion plants.

Geraldo would usually pause midway in his projects, leaving piles of dirt, stones, and plants strewn over the sidewalk as he tottered off. But he was immensely delighted with his vision—"*Vecina!*" he'd yell happily at me as I came out in the morning to survey the destruction. "Neighbor! Look, *que milagro*, it's growing!"—and indefatigable. Martha tried a few times, on the sly, to pull out his rotting onions and some of the rattier geraniums to neaten up the bed, but Geraldo would always be there another morning, on his knees, shaking his head sadly as he replanted the weeds among the garbage. "Somebody messed up your plants last night," he'd say mournfully. "No respect. Don't worry, don't worry, I'll fix it."

Crazily, though, the jade plant was still alive. It had a certain janky charm, especially if I could stay on top of the trash in its branches. And after I'd constructed a border with some scrounged bricks, and Thad, always there with the right tool, had brought a hose out from his garage and watered everything, the hodgepodge under the tree almost looked like a sidewalk garden.

Thad, next door, was a model *vecino*. He was a California native, an artist with the skills of a *Popular Mechanics* handyman. Soon after we moved in, Thad cut a door in the fence between us, making it easy to go back and forth between yards to pick vegetables or flowers. He built a mosaic fire pit for barbecues, and a double-decker tree house for Katie, furnished with a bucket that could be lowered down to receive snacks. We weren't intimate friends, exactly, but we watched each other's kids, fed each other's pets, and shared gossip, keys, and the occasional afternoon beer.

It was Thad who encouraged people on our street to join him in earthquake preparedness training. He and I went to class together at the General Hospital, where the fire department was organizing neighborhood teams and teaching the basics of disaster medicine, search and rescue, and communications. "Neighbors taking care of neighbors," was their slogan: disaster experts knew that in the aftermath of an emergency the authorities would be completely overwhelmed, and people would be on their own to respond block by block.

Even after the drills, my own skills consisted mainly of being able to write down information and boss other people around. Thad, of course, got his ham radio license;

he kept an inventory of shovels, crowbars, pipe wrenches, and plastic sheeting in neatly labeled bins in his basement, ready to go, and soon after our training he bought a 200-gallon cistern for our collective backyard.

Neighbors taking care of neighbors: I was convinced this was the path to earthquake preparedness, and to any meaningful political movement—and in fact to a Christian life. But it made me really nervous, too. Because the closer I got, the higher the stakes became.

I was happy to see Thad coming down the backyard path, clippers in hand, but it took fifteen years before I felt able to cry in front of him. I liked sweeping the sidewalk alongside Don Miguel and chatting over the fence with Linda, but I didn't intend to go out to dinner with her or have him confide in me about his wife's sad decline. I was happy strolling down the block in the role of a generic middle-aged lady stopping to commiserate with Ricardo about the idiocy of city officials, but I wasn't going to spend all my evenings organizing block meetings. I didn't need to get dragged into my neighbors' feuds and tragedies, their intimate lives, the secrets of their souls.

And expressing faith in public, right on my block, was a boundary I wasn't sure I was ready to cross. A few people on the block knew, vaguely, that I had some kind of job working at some kind of church—"Oh," Don Miguel's daughter chirped once, happily, "we're so blessed to have a pastor living next door, and remember Ray in the yellow house, he was a pastor, too, we must be really blessed by so many prayers on both sides!"—but I shied away from any conversation that might lead to more probing questions about exactly what kind of church or pastor. Her comment was embarrassing: I'd prayed *for* my neighbors, but not so much *with* them, and it made me uncomfortable to be praised for a virtue I'd avoided practicing.

I aspired to be the kind of neighbor who knew everyone: trusted and reliable and bursting with old-fashioned civic virtues. I yearned to be in real relationship with others, to grasp the florid social ecology of this one little Mission block, to be fully aware of all the *locura*, the crazy stuff taking place everywhere from the Section 8 apartments two doors down to the newly granite-countered co-op on the corner. ("Five hundred *thousand* dollars?" another inveterately nosy neighbor, a neurotic Colombian hippie lady, whispered to me in shock after we'd tromped through an open house and ogled the way developers had turned a crummy apartment building into a crummy co-op. It was back when $500,000 for a three-bedroom apartment in the Mission seemed like a lot of money.) I wanted to understand, to know, and to be known.

And at the same time I didn't.

Some days I just wanted to be left alone. I wanted the option of not engaging with anyone past a nod and a polite "*adios*." I wanted to be a good *vecina* without leaving my house or letting people like Geraldo help me. In short, I wanted the benefits of the Church, and the solidarity of a movement, without the costs.

In his parable of the Good Samaritan, Jesus makes God's great commandment unequivocal: *love God; love your neighbor*. But like the lawyer who challenges him, I often wished to weasel out of responsibility, hoping to calibrate who, precisely, was my neighbor; how much, exactly, I was required to love which people. I didn't always love my neighbor the drunken gardener, or my neighbor the rich gentrifier, or my unknown neighbor in the yellow house. And I really dreaded the parable's implication that I could be saved by what they had to give.

chapter eight

As I left our house, school was letting out: as usual, a parade of cars and exhaust-belching vans was double-parked along the narrow street, making it impassable. Martha and I had argued about this for years. Her position was that we were lucky, since Katie had been able to walk to the school, and any moms who cared enough to drive their children there were showing admirable involvement with their kids' education, and what was the big deal? It was a minor inconvenience, given how many parents didn't give a shit. My position was that it was just plain rude, and un-civic-minded in the extreme, to double-park blocking somebody else's driveway, namely ours, then leave the car unattended while you wandered into the school to have a chat with the teachers, so everyone trying to get up or down the whole block was gridlocked, unable to move and honking like crazy. Self-righteously, I pointed out that most of the offenders also had exceptionally *large* vehicles. "Whatever," said Martha. "It wouldn't kill you to just wait a few minutes."

I gritted my teeth. The week before, a neighbor from down the street—an unpleasant, older Mexican man always hyper-vigilant about parking infractions—had actually accosted a young mother who had blithely hopped out of her banged-up minvan, leaving the blinkers on, and was strolling toward the school. I didn't hear what he said, but she was outraged, and by the time I arrived at the scene of the crime she'd dialed 911 on her cell and was complaining loudly in Spanish to a bemused operator about his abuse. "*El me estupidó*," she reported, scandalized. "He called me stupid! Please send an officer right now!" The scene had ended with the principal joining me in the street trying to soothe everyone, and the grumpy neighbor, apologetically, borrowing a set of cables to help the double-parker when it turned out, half an hour later, that her battery had died during the argument.

But today he was nowhere to be seen, and my driveway was blocked. I'd never worn a cassock on my own block before, and I was feeling ridiculous in it. I opened the garage door and popped the lock to my trunk, tossing the paper towels in next to the milk crate of thuribles and ashes. It was going to be bad enough to come out as a religious nut a few blocks away, on Mission and 24th, but I couldn't be caught yelling at parents right in front of my house while wearing church drag. Maybe some double-parker would pull out without me having to make a scene, and I wouldn't be spotted by anyone I knew and could just quickly drive away.

To my dismay, though, when I poked my head out of the garage I saw Don Miguel, the patriarch from next door, standing hand in hand with an impatient little girl on the sidewalk in front of Linda's parked blue sedan. He was watching Linda and her husband hoist his wife, the gravely ill Doña Luz, down their concrete stairs. The woman almost perfectly fit Jesus' description of St. Peter—grown old, stretching out her hands, with some-one else fastening a belt around her and taking her where she did not wish to go. Doña Luz wore a hostile expression, as usual, aimed at nobody in particular.

Linda didn't miss a beat. She pointed to me excitedly. "Oh, you have ashes?" she sang out.

Things had been changing next door. Don Miguel and his wife were getting older and feebler, needing more help with daily tasks. I still couldn't recognize all the family members, though Linda had tried to explain the cast of characters in the house more than once. "So there were seven of us kids," she'd say, "and then there's our kids, and the great-grandkids, and also my grandma from Fresno lived here when she got older, and you know my son, he's in New York now? He stayed here for a while to be with his girlfriend and her little boy...." But I could more or less keep track of Don Miguel, since his movements varied little, and he always wore what appeared to be the same SF Giants windbreaker and cap. An excruciatingly bashful retired man with an unreadably weathered face—had he been fifty that first time Gilberto introduced us, nodding hello in front of his garage? Had he been forty? Seventy?—he was followed everywhere by a bitter Pomeranian named "Honey" who watched him jealously as he pushed a broom around. Don Miguel remained intensely preoccupied with sweeping our block, where the gusts of wind he called a *molina*, a windmill, constantly stirred up tormenting storms of Chinese restaurant flyers, Doritos bags, condoms, and leaves. It seemed to be his main focus in life: he seldom made chitchat with me about anything but the garbage on the sidewalk—"*Si, mucha basura*," he'd whisper with a nervous laugh—or occasionally the weather, as it pertained to the sidewalk: *"Mucho viento, heh heh, una molina."*

When I first moved in, Don Miguel was still trudging on daily trips to the Cala supermarket to fetch drinking water in a plastic five-gallon jug. It must have been a holdover habit from his childhood in Mexico; San Francisco's Hetch Hetchy reservoir delivered perfectly fine tap water, pure and unchlorinated. Or maybe it was his attempt to get out of the house. "My dad," Linda confessed to me, "he was so sweet. My mom, well, she wore the pants in the family." Doña Luz almost never emerged from her fortress, except to glare at children or bark at the mailman, and we assumed that Don Miguel also lived in fear of her. In the early years we'd receive gifts of menudo in Tupperware from the neighbors at Christmastime, and Katie would timidly carry back over a paper plate of cookies she'd covered in green and red sprinkles. "Feliz Navidad," she'd squeak in terror if Doña Luz answered the door.

Katie was little then, and I was sure Don Miguel's whole household could hear whenever she cried at night, or when I lost my temper and yelled at her. Most of our contact was with a girl her age named Alejandra and a shrill-voiced boy cousin, a bit older, who called relentlessly across the fence for Katie to come play. Relations cooled after the cousin made an attempt on the life of Katie's rabbit, a docile sack of fur named Simba Cloud, and then that family moved out of the city.

For the next few years, I'd occasionally see Linda in the backyard and a parade of other exhausted parents— a MUNI bus driver in his tan uniform, a nightshift mom with glasses—dropping their kids off before work for Don Miguel and Doña Luz to watch. Simba Cloud died of natural causes and was laid to rest under the plum tree in our garden; Mark, who specialized in writing elegies for pets, offered an ode that began, *"Here lies Simba, regal rabbit / soft of pelt and sweet of habit…"*

Katie and Alejandra grew up and left the Mission. Martha and I noticed a pretty teenager hanging out next door, a deaf girl, kissing and signing with her first boyfriend as they cuddled on the steps by a statue of the Virgin Mary. Then a dark-haired young man in a wheelchair appeared—a grandkid? another cousin?— and angrily parked himself in the open garage door, smoking and refusing to say hello to the neighbors. Occasionally he'd invite groups of friends over to party, loudly, in the backyard. There'd be clouds of smoke, the smell of marijuana and grilling meat, heavyset thuggy boys in red sweatshirts, women shrieking, hip-hop blasting, and a notable absence of elders.

Then suddenly the wheelchair kid was gone, and one day decades of toys, boxes of clothes, and a mattress were hauled out of the garage. "Hey, did you hear Alex passed?" a neighbor told me. "Some kind of infection." I crossed myself.

After a while, we thought that the deaf daughter might have moved back in, with a new boyfriend and a baby. We heard crying at night. *Ma ma mamamama.* The baby howled desperately, and after an excruciating five, ten, fifteen minutes an adult would yell back, in the wordless aria of the deaf, and there'd be more crying, and finally silence.

All along, our own household—me, Katie, Martha, and briefly Katie's father—must have seemed equally opaque to the next-door neighbors, especially since, as I discovered later, they assumed I was related to the previous owners. For years Don Miguel greeted me, warmly, as "Susan" whenever he saw me out front.

But Don Miguel had stopped going to the supermarket for water. His wife, Doña Luz, was on regular dialysis and couldn't really walk; the shrunken, gray-skinned matriarch needed help to get to her garden or down the front stairs. Linda and I had turned into middle-aged women with grown kids and older parents, and now here I was, on Ash Wednesday, standing in front of her house wearing a black cassock and a smudge on my face.

"Oh, good, hi! Ashes, can we get some?" Linda asked again. She was wearing a sweatshirt and a crucifix, and pointed toward the open trunk of my car. It was a clear afternoon, with a little breeze, and I looked over at a crooked olive tree Geraldo tended, suddenly noticing how pretty its leaves were. Doña Luz was on the sidewalk now, waiting for Linda's husband to help her into their car. The little girl was spinning around Don Miguel, humming to herself, her hair studded with barrettes. I drew a blank: every word of the Ash Wednesday service flew out of my head, even as I tried to act as if it were the most natural thing in the world to hold an impromptu religious ritual outdoors with neighbors. "Sure," I said, smiling at Linda. "Um, let me go get some." I went back to my garage and took out a little glass holder of ashes out of my trunk, stalling for time.

Then someone grabbed me from behind. It was Rafael, the sexy, chatty playground coordinator and truant officer I'd known since my daughter was in kindergarten at the school. I turned and he hugged me, hard. "*Mujer*," said Rafael, his spooky, pale green eyes boring into me. "How are you? Sorry about the car blocking your driveway. Gimme some ashes, too?"

I was so busted.

There was nothing dreamy about what happened next. Rafael sprinted off to direct traffic. "Be right back!" he yelled.

I turned and caught Linda's eyes. She lifted her bangs from her forehead and bowed; I walked over and crossed her with ashes and said the words; she pushed the reluctant child forward; and I crossed the little girl's pale face with ashes and said the words. Then Linda's husband, sweating slightly after lifting Doña Luz into their car, came and stood in front of me, baseball cap in his hand. I'd never seen him up this close, not speaking: he dipped his balding head as I fumbled again with the ashes and traced the silky black soot on him. "Remember you're dust," I said, "and to dust you will return." I could hardly breathe. My hand was shaking.

"Thanks," he said, and smiled. "Can you do Linda's mom? We're taking her to the doctor again."

I stepped over to their dented sedan, adorned with a SF Giants bumper sticker and a rosary hanging from the rearview mirror. Doña Luz was in the front seat, and the little girl had climbed in and was wiggling around behind her. I knelt before the open car door. It was so real I wanted to throw up. Doña Luz was staring straight ahead, and I realized that what I'd imagined as her angry glare was only the vacancy of cataracts. "Mama," said Linda gently, "the pastor's going to give you ashes now."

Her skin was thin, a mask over bone, just as it had been on the night last month when I'd heard an ambulance pull up next door. That night, when I came outside barefoot, worried, Linda told me Doña Luz couldn't breathe right and her father was frightened. She and her sister had hovered over the gurney, patting their mom as the paramedics eased her into the ambulance, and then while the sister climbed in beside her, Linda had turned and asked me to pray. "Of course," I said helplessly, and then, on an impulse, had run upstairs to grab a strange little rosary someone made for me in Costa Rica out of white nylon rope and blue beads. "Here," I'd told the old lady, shoving it into her hand. "Take this with you." She'd clutched it without speaking, her expression hidden under the oxygen mask.

Now, kneeling, I touched my thumb to the ashes and

carefully reached up to make the sign of the cross on Doña Luz's forehead. She stared straight ahead.

Forgive me, a sinner.

God forgives you. Forgive me, a sinner.

God forgives you, I reminded myself. But pay attention.

chapter nine

I said good-bye to Linda, gave ashes to Rafael, and let
him stop a gigantic white SUV from occupying our
driveway so that I could back out. Bertie lived a couple
blocks away from me, just a few doors down from the
plaza at 24th and Mission, and now it was going to be my
turn to drive neighbors nuts while I double-parked in
front of his apartment. I'd pick him up, we'd go fetch the
table at Holy Innocents, and then the other ash-givers—I
wasn't entirely sure who was coming—would meet us
back on the plaza.

The invitation had been broad enough: at St. Gregory's
and at a few other Episcopal churches in the Mission area
we announced that ashes would be distributed on 24th
Street beginning around 4 p.m.: anyone who wanted to
participate was welcome. Bertie had recruited a retired

priest and a handful of parishioners from Holy Innocents; a group from Buen Samaritano and St. John's was planning to offer ashes farther down Mission Street, at the corner of 16th. From St. Gregory's I was expecting Kelsey Menehan, who sang soprano in the choir; Vik, the seminarian who'd been at St. Gregory's in the morning; and Vera, the young woman from Texas. I really hoped my friend Rosa Lee Harden, the former vicar at Holy Innocents who had been at our first street service, would also make it: she was fearless and fun.

But there was no way to tell who might show up. As much as I obsessed about neighbors and neighborhoods and neighborliness, it was clear, from experience as well as from Scripture, that "who is my neighbor?" was a question impossible to answer solely by geography or affinity. This Ash Wednesday on the street, I knew I'd be face to face with all kinds of people—strangers, neighbors, and friends alike—who were not necessarily the ones I chose, but the ones God chose for me.

Right around three thirty, I pulled up in front of the little Mission Street apartment, wedged between a bakery and a dingy, old-school Italian restaurant, where Bertie lived with his wife. I phoned, and he came bounding down the stairs, tall and dapper, and slid into the car.

"How do you really pay attention to what the Spirit is doing?" I asked Bertie as we drove away out of the Mission and over to Holy Innocents. Bertie had pink cheeks and a sweet, pale face with swept-back, jet-black hair; in his formal black clericals he looked like a choirboy dressed up as Johnny Cash. "Oh, yeah, yeah, that's the question," he said enthusiastically, as we crossed 24th Street heading west up the hill. "Because we don't do it very well. God is happening all the time, but we focus on less important things."

Even before he'd helped me launch our first Ash Wednesday street services in 2010, Bertie had found a mission in the Mission, where people like Mark had long been creating a vibrant, messy arts movement. Bertie was a successful DJ and punk drummer from Austin, with a serious grudge against the commercial music industry. "They were perverting what we did into a culture of hipsterism, a commodity," he explained. "It was revolting to see record labels start selling affiliation to our subculture, with guys who had the same tight pants and combat boots as us turned into the new Don Henley. So we looked for a new way of being punk."

He moved to the Mission in 1999, settling into a punk house on 24th Street. "It was a constantly changing place," he remembered. "There was another DJ, a crazy party guy; two women who ran a record label; a girl who later died of a heroin overdose; a bunch of skateboarders who liked to scratch yuppies' cars on principle.

"We were loud, we wore crazy thrift-store clothes and went Dumpster diving. Then *that* scene became valued by marketers. There was a transition from being cool in a punk-rock way to being cool in a mainstream way. Suddenly, chucking all of it and walking around in a priest suit seemed real."

I could see why Bertie made some people nervous. On the one hand, he was everything older Christians could dream of in a young priest: articulate, polite, married to a beautiful and brilliant woman; well-dressed, well-educated at UC Berkeley and Oxford; media-savvy. He was completely respectful of tradition: his clergy mentor in San Francisco was the rector of an Anglo-Catholic parish known for its flawless, stylized liturgy. Plus he was connected with the cool music-scene kids; his bishop, impressed, had allowed him to run a late-night dance party called Episcodisco in Grace Cathedral. Bertie was the kind of hip priest you could imagine being held up as "the future of the Church."

And yet Bertie was a wild card: he was a real believer.

He wasn't a go-with-the-flow liberal, a company man, or even remotely ironic. Just as he'd rejected the music industry, he might at any point reject the religion industry. For all his excellent grooming and manners Bertie was still a punk at heart—a punk for God.

Since he was a toddler, Bertie had thought hard about God. His mother brought him to Chimayo, the Roman Catholic shrine in New Mexico known for the popular devotion of pilgrims who collect its dirt for healing. "The place was very dark and cool and protected, as if the blazing sun and the harsh world couldn't get in," he remembered. "There were all these strange wooden statues, dressed in elaborate fabric outfits. You could sit or kneel at the altar rail, or go to an area filled with crutches and eyeglasses, and then go from there to a big dirt pit." He paused. "When I was little, Chimayo was the first place I felt that experience of awe and trust in God's perfect peace and goodness, that knowledge of God's love."

It never left him. When he was four and his parents divorced, Bertie's mother took him to live for six months in a Buddhist monastery. At seven, he told his atheist father that he wanted to be a priest. At ten, his sister gave him a Dead Kennedys record, and at twelve he got his first drum set and began playing in Latin and rock bands. By the time he'd left Austin and was living in the Mission, Bertie was making electronic music, DJ-ing, party-promoting, dancing all night, drinking, hanging out in clubs—and going to church every Sunday while studying theology. He was ordained as a priest in the Episcopal Church when he was thirty. "It's a miracle," he said. "I mean, you keep on being a selfish jerk, but there's this secret reservoir you can keep going back to, where you can see the Spirit praying within you."

It *is* a miracle, I thought: how the Spirit could move without warning through a life; how Bertie and I, with our different but equally irregular pasts, would move to the same city and wind up, of all things, Episcopalians. And now in 2012, for the third year in a row, we were preparing to pray together and offer ashes on the streets of the neighborhood we both lived in.

Here's how our new tradition got started. Back in 2009, at the urging of the central diocesan office where Bertie was then working, Episcopal churches in the Mission area met to discuss possible joint projects. Bertie's mentor at Church of the Advent suggested creating an outdoor processional liturgy as "a public act of repentance" for homelessness and street violence, and holding it on Good Friday. "You know, the Anglo-Catholics love processions," Bertie said. "So folks from Advent, St. John's, Holy Innocents, and St. Gregory's, and I think the Franciscans, did that 2009 Good Friday walk."

That day we covered a lot of ground, walking from the courtyard of St. John's at one end of the Mission to the steps of Holy Innocents at the other, stopping to chant prayers at places where people had been murdered, or at sites of suffering the group designated as "stations of the cross." We prayed at the police station, in a garbage-filled park where a boy had been shot, in front of a homeless shelter. Some of our group—about forty men and women and a couple of small children—chatted as we strolled, while others seemed lost in their own meditations. A nun, in her brown Franciscan habit, carried a large photograph of a bound, blindfolded, kneeling Iraqi prisoner with a duct-taped wound in his side; two women in sweatshirts took turns carrying a heavy cross, and a couple of thurifers censed storefronts and passersby enthusiastically. Most onlookers smiled, and a few fell in step with us at different points, joining in the hymns. In this neighborhood, an outdoor Good Friday commemoration wasn't particularly unusual.

Still, I felt awkward when the procession crossed paths with people I knew: a caseworker at the homeless shelter, a guy from our food pantry outside the check-cashing place on 16th Street, a friend of Mark's at the achingly hip Ritual Coffee. I'd been a member of St. Gregory's for almost a decade by then, and a leader in its liturgies, but what I thought of as my church life and my "real" life didn't usually bump into each other so publicly.

I was assigned to chant a prayer in Spanish at a boarded-up gas station, and when we got there I leaned dry-mouthed against the chain-link fence in a borrowed cassock, feeling self-conscious and fraudulent. I wasn't clergy, I wasn't a native Spanish speaker, I'd never before been part of a Good Friday procession, and in fact I couldn't remember all the stations of the cross in order. But then, as the group started walking again, a sweaty black guy with a shaved head came up and grabbed my sleeve urgently. "Mother!" he blurted out, "I want to come with you all but I have to go somewhere in a hurry, can you bless me?" He bent in close, sorrowful and dope-sick, and suddenly it seemed silly to be concerned with how others might see me. "You're just out there," Bertie said, "as an icon of the Church, and people come before you in humility and bow their heads, and it really isn't about you at all."

The next year, 2010, Bertie gave me a call. He was still working for the diocese, but he kept an ear out for what was happening in the Mission. He'd heard that Will, the chaplain, was planning to hold Ash Wednesday services at the General Hospital and that I'd been talking with local churches about the possibility of offering ashes outside. Someone suggested Bertie and I should get together and plan the liturgies, since I was "determined" to do it at the corner of 24th and Mission. He was terrified. "I mean, I *live* at Twenty-fourth and Mission," Bertie told me, "right there, less than half a block away, and every day I walk past these fundamentalists screaming: 'The blood of Jesus is real, you must repent, Jesus loves you.' All of which I agree with, you know, but…"

"I know," I said.

"I *detest* the way they give the message," Bertie said fiercely. "It's really challenging to think about being in the heart of my community, trying to reclaim the public language of sin and repentance from the fundamentalists. So much of my life has been distinguishing myself from them." He stopped and then continued in a gentler voice.

"They must sometimes feel as awkward as we do," Bertie said.

"I wonder," I said.

I was used to the unease many progressive Christians felt about "reclaiming the language of sin and repentance," and I struggled with it as a preacher. People who had spent years condemned by various denominations for being gay boys or sexually active girls, or for expressing doubt, and had found their way back to a church that could accept them as they were didn't tend to appreciate hearing a lot more about wretchedness or Jesus' blood.

Like most converts, I had an annoying tendency to talk about Jesus just a little bit more than anybody else wanted to hear. But sin: that was different. I preached about sin because I believed in mercy. And I believed in mercy because I knew how quickly even my stupidest, most ordinary sins could drag me into a spiral of misery. I'd be mean, or lazy, or selfish, and feel bad about it, and so I'd become meaner, less able to get up, less interested in thinking about anybody else. That inward-driving force, which takes the mind prisoner and locks the soul in solitary confinement, nourishes even the smallest sin and makes living with it, essentially, hell.

And the only way out of it, on Ash Wednesday as on

any day, is repentance. Not feeling bad, but changing. Not pouring ashes on your head in a fit of self-loathing, but allowing Jesus to gently spit into a handkerchief and scrub off your face.

And so I'd experienced Jesus' unexpected lifting of a burden; the freedom that could flood into my sorry heart from a larger, sacred heart. It was calling me to get out of myself and into the holy city, into actual relationships with other people and with God. Because out there on the streets, as those crazy preachers shout, startling the pigeons, is the Revelation: *"Behold, I am making all things new!"*

Early in 2010, Bertie and I arranged to meet in the plaza, checking it out and making notes for how to do our first Ash Wednesday street liturgy there. We sat on the little ledge that ran by a chain-link fence, near where the salsa band usually played, and studied the scene as commuters rose out of the depths of the BART station, waves of middle school kids swept along the sidewalk, and panhandlers wove in and out of the crowd. It felt oddly peaceful, amid the car radios blaring and buses roaring and periodic shouts from vendors hawking SF Giants caps.

Perhaps hoping to distinguish ourselves from the fundamentalists, Bertie refused to even consider using an amp on Ash Wednesday. "One, amplifiers always sound terrible," he said. "Two, you're supposed to have a permit. Three, you can't drown out the background noise anyway. We just need to make a sound that stands out."

We came up with an outline for a street service that afternoon. I was concerned with the space and how we'd use it; I didn't want to just take a standard indoor liturgy and transport it outside. Bertie, ever the traditionalist, wanted to open with the blessing of ashes from the Book of Common Prayer. But ever the cool Mission party promoter, too, he thought we could grab people's attention by having a black-robed procession appear on the plaza as three Brazilian drummers he knew—"Awesome guys!" he exclaimed—pounded out an opening anthem to signal that something really exciting was about to start.

Over the next few days Bertie drew up a script. In his first draft, he suggested we walk from Holy Innocents to the plaza in complete silence. "The procession, in its haunting silence and gravity, should communicate the solemnity of the day," he wrote. "If those on the street attempt to speak to one of us, we will respectfully, non-verbally communicate that we are maintaining silence with either a finger held up to the lips or a bow to them with hands folded in a gesture of prayer."

"Are you fucking kidding?" I thought to myself when I read his draft.

"Um, Bertie," I told him when we met, trying to be slightly more tactful, "I think that's a little insider-y. First of all, how are you going to have a conversation with people if you don't *talk* with them? And why in the world would we do *mime* on the streets to explain ourselves?"

"Okay," Bertie said immediately, humbly. "You're right." But I was warming up. "It's like that stupid Episcopal secret language they use in fussy churches where if you don't want communion, you're supposed to signal it by crossing your arms over your chest and bowing, and maybe blinking three times, as if someone who's in church for the first time is gonna intuit how to do these secret gestures instead of just saying, like a normal person, 'no thanks.' You really want to do that crap in the Mission? It's so arrogant."

"Okay, okay," Bertie said patiently. "Anything else?"

Winning an argument always made me even bossier. "Well, we could use copal for incense and cense the four corners of the plaza at the beginning of the service," I began. *Copal*, the yellowish resin used by Aztecs to bless the four directions of the world, still fills Mexican Catholic churches with the smell of prayers more ancient than Jesus; it marks the opening of a sacred liturgy in both traditions.

"*Copal*," said Bertie. "People will recognize the smell."

I calmed down. Bertie was my comrade, and he knew what he was doing. He'd said he'd print some signs and postcards to hand out, and find a card table to set up as the altar. I'd bring the *copal* and thuribles. We'd both put out a call to neighborhood churches for volunteers, and he'd round up the drummers. We made a little checklist: prayerbook, matches, ashes...

"Duct tape," I said firmly. It was not for nothing I'd gone to those NERT classes with Thad.

And so, on Ash Wednesday, 2010, we did our first offering of ashes in the street. About a dozen people volunteered to take part: Rosa Lee Harden offered to gather everyone at Holy Innocents, where she was serving as the vicar, and to lead the procession to the plaza where Bertie would be waiting with the drummers. A tough, funny, politically savvy priest from Mississippi who'd battled inside and outside the Episcopal Church for years on issues of inclusion, Rosa Lee was a good friend of Paul's. She was blond, with a straightforward, unfussy manner; she liked to drink bourbon and laugh loudly and throw big, messy dinner parties. Rosa Lee didn't hesitate to take risks. "Let's go!" she said when she heard our plan. "How many cassocks will you need to borrow?"

Holy Innocents was a small, old-fashioned wooden church, standing on a hill at the western border between the Mission and the far more upscale neighborhood of Noe Valley. Maybe a third of its members lived in the Mission, almost all of them white: artists, techies, and upper-middle-class young families, part of what Rosa Lee called "the incredibly complex demographic" of the neighborhood. It was a socially progressive and liturgically mainstream congregation; as Rosa Lee admitted, sometimes it felt a little predictable. "As a clergyperson," she told me, "you tend to know what's gonna happen inside your church. Surprise is rare. Ash Wednesday at Holy Innocents is small and by the book; it's the same people showing up every year in the same way. Sometimes it gets hard to see the life in the ritual."

"Here we go!" said Rosa Lee in her throaty voice when everyone was assembled. She smiled warmly and gave me a big hug. I was queasy and thrilled. We began singing a repetitive chant and took off down 24th Street, trying to dodge overhanging street trees and keep from tripping on the cracked sidewalks. There were a couple of priests participating and a few seminarians, but even the professionals weren't necessarily used to stomping through city streets in long black robes, and our group moved a little awkwardly. Medieval processions hadn't needed to contend with traffic lights.

We arrived at the plaza. "Hey, did you know today is Ash Wednesday?" a white hipster shouted into his phone, staring at our procession and trying to snap a picture. "No shit!"

Bertie, wearing his clerical collar, was using the duct tape to post two large handwritten signs to the fence. *Life is Very, Very, Very Short* said one, and the other read *More Forgiveness*. Near his feet was a stack of postcards with a black-and-white drawing of someone like one of the drag-queen nuns from the Sisters of Perpetual Indulgence, wearing a cross of ashes on her forehead. The caption, in Spanish and English, announced that "the Episcopal Church is pro-immigrant, pro-equality, and anti-hater."

The burly Brazilian drummers, three of them, were going wild. I fished a few sticky crumbs of *copal* out of my pocket and dropped them on the coals in my thurible, and then our whole group walked deliberately around the corners of the busy plaza, censing east and west, north and south with clouds of smoke. We returned to the card table and gathered in a clump before it; the drummers pounded out a last barrage, then stopped. My ears rang with the sudden absence of percussion.

"O God," began Bertie, chanting in a serious, clear voice and looking up toward heaven, "you made us from the dust of the earth. Grant that these ashes may be a sign of our mortality and penitence..."

He was holding a baby-food jar full of ashes in both hands, raising it high in front of him. Now bystanders were edging nearer to see what we were doing, and a seminarian with long, curly black hair addressed everyone. "Let us kneel before the God who made us," she said to the crowd.

I knelt. I bent over and pressed my forehead to the sidewalk, the whole rush of this neighborhood, its crazy beauty and apparent hopelessness, flooding my heart. I'd walked through the plaza the day two teenagers were shot a block away. I'd seen someone OD in the subway entrance. I'd come here busy and distracted on the way to the library with my lover and five-year-old daughter; I'd eaten tacos, chatted with beggars, and laughed with friends on this holy ground. "Lord," I whispered, "have mercy."

Now it was 2012, and we were getting ready for another Ash Wednesday on the same streets. Bertie sat beside me in the passenger seat as I drove up 24th Street, past the plaza and library toward Holy Innocents. "That first Ash Wednesday..." he reminisced, looking out the window at an outdoor café where a group of men was playing cards. It was hard to keep track of all the details from previous years: when, exactly, did Bertie bless the Peruvian guy with the scar? When did that Italian lady offer me a sandwich? "I'd just been ordained for about eleven months, and really, all I remember is I was so scared."

"And the next time, was it different?" I asked. Since 2010, a lot had changed in his life: Bertie had left his diocesan job and become the priest-in-charge of both Holy Innocents and St. John's, dividing his time between the congregations at either end of the Mission.

Bertie mused. He was wearing extremely stylish pointy black boots, and his suit was perfectly creased.

"You know those postcards I made," he said, "along with all the explanations? I think the first year I was a new priest, and I saw the whole street service maybe as more of a great PR opportunity, like 'Hey, check out the Episcopal Church, we're not like those other Christians, you'll like us.'

"But then," Bertie said, and shot me a smile, "by 2011, maybe I didn't have quite so much to prove. I didn't think we needed postcards. Or drummers. Or even the entire ceremony of blessing the ashes, either—you were right, it wasn't about taking a regular church service and doing it outdoors, it was about doing an outdoor service. And the immediacy was *amazing*. Giving ashes just became about the real experience for me and each person I touched: our experience of God."

I told Bertie about a friend's comment upon seeing photos from Ash Wednesday of the two of us "calling the Mission to repentance," as my friend nicely put it. "The advantage of being a religious fanatic is that you get to do stuff like that without fear," he mused. "Sort of like being a punk—you can get drunk in the day and shoot up in the street without worrying about what the neighbors think."

I still worried about the neighbors, though, I confessed

to Bertie. Despite our previous Ash Wednesday experiences, I was anxious about this year's service, the one we were about to begin: I felt exposed. Punk as he was, Bertie admitted he did, too. "Sometimes in the Mission I run into old music friends who say, 'Bertie! What are you doing in that priest outfit?' and I say, 'Well, um, I'm a priest,' and they just look at me with *horror*."

We laughed. "You live right here, too," Bertie said to me. "Don't you find it hard to be out in the Mission in front of all your neighbors?"

"Yes," I said. "I do."

"And especially," he continued, "on Ash Wednesday, it's crazy: it's like getting a face tattoo for an hour. The whole day is wild. It's such a brief, sacramental moment when you impose ashes, under sixty seconds, but each time your faith is so visible and out there."

"Yes," I said, pulling up in front of the bright red doors of Holy Innocents. "Well, here we go again."

Bertie unlocked the church and chatted with his friendly deacon for a minute while I phoned Will at the General and left a message asking him to keep an eye out for Mr. Claws. Maybe, I thought, the key would be just to repent of my constant multitasking and focus on doing one thing at a time. But I checked my voice mail any-

125

way. Then Bertie pulled a folding card table out of the closet, packed it into the car next to my crates, and with all the supplies finally together, we headed back down to the Mission.

It was nearly four. I worried that Vera and Kelsey might have arrived at the plaza already and wouldn't find us there. Kelsey was funny and grounded and pretty unflappable: a therapist, she'd done counseling with victims of trauma in places like Kosovo and Gaza, so I figured she could handle it if we were a little late. Vera always seemed calm, but I wanted to be there when she arrived. I'd learned, finally, why this day was so important to Vera. A few years ago, on Ash Wednesday, her older sister Audrey had killed herself.

"I was planning to read in the Ash Wednesday service at my church in Texas," Vera said, recounting the story, "and was getting on my bicycle when the phone rang. It was my dad, and he said, 'Audrey's no longer with us.'"

Vera had gone back into her house and collapsed. "I was wailing, pounding the walls; I fell down on the ground, saying maybe it was an accident, maybe she's still alive. I called my dad back to see if it was real."

Vera spoke carefully, deliberately, as if she were folding precious handwritten letters into tiny packets. "It was real," she said. "Audrey had taken her life, jumping from the top of the parking garage at the hospital. She'd died by the time my parents got there. We found out"—Vera made a small sound, a moan—"Audrey received the ashes. A chaplain in the hospital gave her ashes.

"I couldn't speak," Vera said. "I went home to my parents' house, my brother was there, my dad was on the phone with organ donation. Nothing made sense. I remember writing one sentence in my journal: *from dust we came to dust we shall return*. It was what I call my first Ash Wednesday, when Audrey died.

"That year there was a really early Easter. It was such an offense. I couldn't bear it: how could Lent be just like the blink of an eye, when Lent is the world we live in?"

I could see the outline of her dead sister in Vera's steady, suffering gaze. "Ash Wednesday is like a homecoming for me," she said remorselessly. "It's the most honest of days. It's a mystery, a sitting-with." She let out her breath. "A sitting with the dark. It is bearing witness to the dark."

Now, as Bertie and I pulled up on 24th Street by the plaza, I thought I could make out Vera and Kelsey and someone in a clerical collar: it looked as if the ash-giving group might be gathering over by the entrance to the BART. As usual, the plaza was full, with scores of people striding through it purposefully and dozens hanging out around the perimeter. A bunch of the hanging-out regulars were smoking and gabbing by the bus stop, and I waved at them. "Hey," I called, rolling down the window, "can you give Father a hand?" Bertie got out of the car, and he and one of the guys unloaded the table and my milk crates full of gear. "I'm gonna go park," I said. "Be right back, and then we can start."

chapter ten

Although Bertie and I hadn't known it in 2010 when we held our first Ash Wednesday service outdoors in the Mission, other churches around the country had also been experimenting with what they called "Ashes to Go." Over the next few years, we kept hearing more stories about the new meanings Ash Wednesday reveals when it takes place outside of church buildings. Witness, suffering, mortality; solidarity, prayer, repentance: everything that happens inside of church can happen outside, but it often looks different. "In the street," as Rosa Lee noted, "the Holy Spirit is working overtime. Reactions are coming out of you, and at you, from all directions. The breath of God is present in a different way—there's no way to be jaded, it's all new."

Benjamin Stewart, a dean at the Lutheran School of

Theology, wrote in an article about public liturgy for *Christian Century* magazine, "All religious ritual is in a sense strange, and this strangeness is part of what generates ritual's theological power...when walls are stripped away...the significance of the ritual is no longer interpreted by the church's physical structure, but unfolds in a symbolically noisy public setting. The range of possible interpretations of the rite—and the number and diversity of interpreters—increases dramatically."

There were different interpretations, even among the people who did it, about the purpose of holding services in the street. Some of the churches we heard or read about seemed determined to make Ash Wednesday services more "accessible" and quick. "If people can grab breakfast on the go, or pay a bill from their cell phone," one priest was quoted in a newspaper article as saying, "why shouldn't they be able to get their ashes in a flash?" Others were interested in reaching people who had fallen away from attending church or who might be encouraged to learn about the tradition for the first time: they handed out promotional flyers with information about their denomination or their indoor services, much as Bertie had done the first time we took ashes outside.

In Ohio, a parish offered drive-through ashes; in various towns in New England, volunteers met commuters at train stations with banners and brief outdoor liturgies. In St. Louis, Teresa Danieley, the Episcopal priest who'd launched "Ashes to Go" in 2007 with an ecumenical group of clergy, explained that the church was "bringing spirit, belief, and belonging out from behind church doors, and into the places where we go every day." With her help, a few years later, the Episcopal Church Foundation published an "Ashes to Go Guide" including sample handouts, liturgies, and written prayers that began to be used by churches around the country.

But inevitably there was criticism, too. After I wrote about our 2011 experiences on the religious news site Episcopal Café, one priest commented that he was "troubled" by any Ash Wednesday service that didn't include "pointed emphasis" on the invitation to name and repent of sins. "Taking the imposition of ashes out of a liturgical context that includes scripture readings, the invitation to a holy Lent, and the litany of penitence, there is no insistence on the reality of sin or any call to repentance," he wrote. "Without the Ash Wednesday liturgy, the imposition of ashes becomes a kind of implicit affirmation of persons as they are." Another reader said that giving out ashes on the street was "a sorry basis for faith and leaves those receiving it with the idea that all rites and rituals are a form of mojo."

Bertie heard the criticism but thought the Church was perhaps not getting the point. "Priests assume—*I* assumed—'Oh, regular people don't have a full realization of the profundity of their mortality, people on the street don't get it.'" He sighed. "So you receive those ashes on your forehead and say you don't understand the ritual... but it's not about the ritual itself, it's about God's grace. And *nobody* comprehends God's grace. You just have to humble yourself to receive it."

Rosa Lee was blunt. "That's just ridiculous," she declared categorically, wrapping the sting of the words in her Southern drawl. "Deciding it's not real unless it happens in the traditional way—that says you think you can limit what God's doing."

Paul agreed. "God is all over the place," he said simply. Inside church buildings or outside, what mattered to him about worship was less tradition for its own sake than "our own desire to be made new. To understand more and more of God, by opening ourselves to those unlike us."

And that meant more than liturgical innovation. As well as offering ashes in public, a coalition of Mission clergy and churches argued that Ash Wednesday's call for repentance could include public prayers for political change, too. One year, Bertie had gone to the downtown headquarters of Wells Fargo with the coalition to urge churches to withdraw their parish funds from big banks "that failed the community by squeezing the poor while accepting taxpayer bailouts." He held up a check showing St. John's withdrawal of funds from Wells Fargo, as another priest, a community organizer, sprinkled ashes on the ground and called for the bank to put a freeze on foreclosures. "It seems appropriate as we enter into this season of penitence," the priest suggested, "that we invite those who separated themselves from the community to repent with us." The protesters likened the divestment campaign to early Christianity's very public ritual of reconciliation of penitents, one that echoed in Ash Wednesday's liturgies: *Is this not the kind of fast I have chosen, to loose every yoke and not turn your back on your own flesh and blood?*

Bertie and Rosa Lee were not insurgents, any more than Paul was. All of them really loved the Church, even with its frequently neurotic demands for order. They loved the

Book of Common Prayer, with its confession that "we have followed too much the devices and desires of our own hearts." They loved the stone arches and solemn echoes of cathedrals like Grace, at the top of Nob Hill in San Francisco, and the smooth wooden pews at little buildings like Holy Innocents: "this set-aside physical space," as Bertie said, "that gives you a connection to the eternal and the infinite, so you can grasp something un-graspable." They loved their parishioners, including the impossible ones, loved crossing themselves, loved vesting for services and the smell of incense. They were enthu-siasts for bringing people inside church buildings, to be transformed by participating in Christian community. As Rosa Lee said, "Where else are you gonna go and have people tell you the truth out loud?"

And yet my priest friends wanted more. As each of them had been ordained, a bishop proclaimed the beau-tiful words from the Book of Common Prayer: "*O God of unchangeable power and eternal light: look favorably on your whole Church, that wonderful and sacred mystery... let the whole world see and know that things which were cast down are being raised up, and things which had grown old are being made new...*" I wondered if my friends, even as they promised to be loyal to the tradition and obedient to the authorities, heard that wild, Gospel promise buzzing in their ears: *all* things, even the wonderful and sacred mystery of the Church, are being made new. And if that prayer—so traditional and so subversive at the same time—made them unable to settle for worship-by-the-book and forced them to spend their lives looking for what else God might be up to.

My own relationship with the Church—as a layperson and an impatient, unschooled, opinionated Jesus freak—was different, but equally complicated. Once, when I was complaining about a long, boring cathedral service with its deafening blasts of grandiose organ music, Paul pointed out that perhaps the style of the music wasn't my real objection. "You just don't like church all that much," Paul observed. I must have looked shocked. "You have an evangelist's heart," he explained tactfully.

"What does *that* mean?" I demanded defensively. I felt I spent an inordinate number of my waking hours in church, preaching and composing newsletters and writing liturgies and moving sacred furniture around and praying with parishioners in crisis. I got mail from the Church Pension Fund, I had a desk in a church office, I knew how to talk to other pastors and which Psalms to pull out for a funeral and how to clean candle wax off vestments. I thought I was getting pretty good at doing church, for an amateur.

"Well," said Paul not much less cryptically, "there are priests of the Church, and there are priests of Jesus." He looked at me kindly. "It's really hard to be a priest of Jesus without the Church," he said.

Indeed, it was tempting to imagine myself, romantically, as a solitary "priest of Jesus," unencumbered by and superior to the Church that baptized me and gave me communion. It was tempting to think I'd figured out how to be a Christian—a better, smarter, less boring kind of Christian—all by myself. But I had to admit this was impossible.

Still, my life at St. Gregory's hadn't endeared me to churchgoing so much as it had allowed me to fall precipitously in love with what God was doing in the world. My experiences inside that beautiful building opened my eyes to the holy everywhere: strangers offering each other banana bread in line at the food pantry, Martha bringing a bunch of wet, white calla lilies to our next-door neighbors, a woman giving Mr. Claws a cup of water in the pharmacy waiting room. I'd learned, by immersion in the ordinary streets of this larger, unhoused Church, that things which were cast down—a strange gardener, a weeping teenage mother, a sick old man—were being raised up. I'd glimpsed, disturbingly, that things which had grown old—my prejudices and self-righteousness, for example—were being made new, whether I liked it or not.

It hurt sometimes to see God out in the holy city, where suffering and dying were real, where I couldn't manage experience or make it into an allegory. But I wanted so badly to get beyond the tastefully enclosed museum of religious life. I wanted to stand on the kind of holy ground that wasn't curated by church professionals, where a burning bush could blaze forth in defiance of safety regulations and outside of regular office hours. I wanted to walk arm in arm with other people, listening for the strangeness and power of God's voice on streets where the volume wasn't going to be decorously muted, where we might find ourselves upset or offended, where we might truly *see and know that all things are being brought to their perfection, by Him through whom all things were made.* I yearned to pray that prayer smack in the middle of the Mission, unafraid. And there, as the bearded gnome-lady had instructed me, to "say the name of Jesus." To evangelize.

To be sure, the brutal, crusading history of Christianity presents any would-be evangelist with a very low bar: don't convert others by violence, bullying, blaming, lying, or selling. But the real challenge of Christian evangelism for me is about how to *attend*. It's the question we kept encountering in the streets of the Mission on Ash Wednesdays, as hundreds and hundreds of people came forward asking to receive ashes: how to see what God is already doing. How to be with other people and let *their* relationships with God evangelize *us*.

As the Orthodox theologian Demetrios Constantelos points out, in a commentary upending many assumptions about evangelism: "It is the Spirit which moves where it wills, whose presence and operation is everywhere and all-encompassing. The Spirit of God may not be where one would like to see it and it may be where one refuses to see it. Thus it is impossible to define the boundaries of God's people."

There is no boundary, really, except the very thin layers of skin touching skin, my thumb and a stranger's forehead, made slippery with the ashes that signify our shared mortality. And those ashes, like all blessings, are not "imposed" by one person on another, but mess everyone up. They unleash a power that flows back and forth, creating space for the good news to be revealed between us.

The good news, the *evangelium* we go outdoors to proclaim, isn't rooted in morals: do this, then God will approve. Nor does the good news offer a magic, protective amulet: most people in the Mission, as everywhere, suffer and have their prayers go unanswered. The good news isn't one more self-help proposition, a path toward becoming a better and nicer person, a way to help others or even to build community. It takes something weirder and harsher to push me out of my private life and onto my knees on the sidewalk.

The good news of Ash Wednesday, the blessing so many people seek so fervently, comes from acknowledging the truth: that we are all going to die. That these busy lives, full of eating and drinking and buying and talking on our cell phones, are going down to the dust. That despite the lies of the culture, the fantasy that money or objects will keep us alive, we mortals are just mortal and connected to one another through that raw, fleshly fact. And Christian evangelism, what we're doing out there on the street, proclaims publicly that we are all also connected to God, past death.

"The year after my sister died on Ash Wednesday," Vera said, "my pastor put ashes on my forehead and told me I would return to dust. It was so comforting. I whispered, 'I'll come, Audrey.' It was as if all my grief and separation would be put to rest. Someday, all separations would be…dust. That felt like a blessing."

The experiences of Ash Wednesday on the street don't make me any more chipper about the prospect of my own death, or more accepting of the unbearable thought that my own beloved daughter or mother will eventually die: I remain glad to stumble through my days in denial. I certainly can't hang out piously on a street corner evangelizing my neighbors with a promise of "eternal life" as if I never have doubts or dread. I trust—at moments, I just *know*—that what Paul said is absolutely true: the worst thing, death, is not the last thing. But the odd contours of Jesus' resurrection usually appear in my mind like clouds—coming into focus, drifting away, and leaving just little puffs of calm in an empty sky. It takes the gritty physicality of ashes, the brushed touch of a hand, the racket of urban streets to make Christian faith real for me. And it takes other people—strangers, neighbors, and friends—sharing their lives with me in the presence of death to complete the blessing.

I once did a funeral service for a stranger—one of the aging *salseros* who play on weekends at the plaza at 24th and Mission, slamming out their hot, syncopated sound for tips. A young Chicana social worker called my St. Gregory's office, trying to find someone to lead a service in Spanish for the musician, nicknamed Chucho. It would be at the housing project where Chucho had lived, two blocks from the plaza. His friends didn't go to church, exactly, but said they felt the need of a "respectful" way to remember him.

Like most of the other *salseros*, Chucho was a Puerto Rican from New York who'd settled in the Mission decades ago and had been making music at the plaza ever since. The group stuck together despite divorces from fed-up women tired of hauling babies to the Laundromat alone on Saturday mornings while the guys set up their congas; despite earnest white girls trying to establish organic farmers' markets on their turf; despite Norteño drug dealers and overzealous cops chasing them away; despite competition from street preachers, Mexican *rockeros*, vendors hawking Frida Kahlo T-shirts. They kept playing through it all until Chucho's heart gave out.

In a drab little common room next to the housing project's courtyard, we set up a bench to use as an altar for the service and put a box with Chucho's ashes on it, draped in a Puerto Rican flag. I looked at the assembled mourners: guys wearing *guayaberas* and slacks, a few women in nice blouses, some old Latino hippies with ponytails, a couple of young adults with polished shoes. I was trying to look respectable in my own gray suit. "All of us, alive or dead, are part of God's life," I began, a little shyly. Then I spoke the words of the Kontakion, the burial hymn used in the Book of Common Prayer: "*All of us go down to the dust, but even at the grave we make our song, alleluia,*" and invited people to share their memories.

The bandleader, an earnest man, went first, bowing his head and clasping his hands. In polite, formal Spanish, he spoke of meeting Chucho in the Mission "to explore our musical heritage." Then others started coming forward with less idealized and funnier stories. "Chucho, he always had a lady," one heavyset man observed, impressed.

"He got around." A dignified, upright African American woman, the mother of his son, stood. "He wasn't a bad guy, Chucho," she said, obviously struggling to not speak ill of the dead. "Not always the most...most mature individual, but he did love his music." And then the son, rumpled and distressed, hugged his mom and tried to say a few words, and the other old musicians clapped for him as he wept into his sleeve. I called people up to the altar, where they took turns kneeling to make their own devotions and good-byes, kissing the picture of Chucho, touching the box of ashes.

"Jesus—in heaven or wherever, may Jesus love him," said one of the *salseros*, crossing himself. That was the last word.

And then we sang. I didn't stay for the hours of jamming that followed, which the *salseros* had clearly been waiting for, but told the bandleader I'd see them all soon, on 24th Street and Mission. "*Que Dios le bendiga*," he said sweetly. "May God bless you." Walking home, I crossed the plaza. It was empty of music now, just filled with the usual random collection of bums and junkies, working mothers and bus passengers. And Chucho with the resurrected Jesus—in heaven or wherever.

It's easier to see the connection between death and resurrection at St. Gregory's, where it's made explicit by the very design of the church. The baptismal font is set outside the building, its waters pouring down from a great split-open rock. Right next to it, cut into the hill, is a columbarium that holds the ashes of the dead, adorned with a mosaic image of Jesus rising out of the tomb.

Each Ash Wednesday we cross one another's foreheads with ashes, remembering our mortality. And forty days later, each Easter, we go out to the baptismal font singing the ancient Christian troparion: *Christ is risen from the dead, trampling down death by death, and on those in the tombs bestowing life.*

We press our bodies together, watching the ritual. In the font's dark water, the newly baptized die with Christ to their old selves. They are lifted up, born again with Christ to new life, and their wet foreheads sealed with another cross, this time of chrism from a small jar. The ointment smells like tiger balm and is pressed firmly into the skin. "You are sealed by the Holy Spirit in baptism," the priest says, tracing the cross on a forehead, "and marked as Christ's own forever." Sealed and marked as belonging to the one who tramples down death. Sealed and marked so that water cannot finally drown, nor flesh be forever reduced to ashes.

Then the holy tiger balm is rinsed off, a hand towel proffered, and—if my own experience is any indication—the lofty baptismal vows, "to forgive as you are forgiven, to renounce all evil, to love and serve your neighbor as yourself," are routinely broken. Sisters die, or the radio reports horrific massacres in other countries, or you lie there late at night wondering about the lesion on your face, or whether your neighbor will make it through surgery.

Yet each year, there is the chance again to bend your head on Ash Wednesday. And each year, as the ashes are imposed and the fact of death spoken aloud, the crossing also retraces the other, baptismal marking: the indelible seal of Easter that makes our mortal bodies part of a living one.

Just a month before Ash Wednesday in 2011, I was at home in the Mission when I got a call from Sanford, our music director. "I think it's happening," he said, his voice shaky. I drove across the bridge to Oakland, and when I got to Sanford's little yellow stucco house he was sitting on a couch in the living room next to the body of his partner, George, who had just died.

Sanford and I rubbed our thumbs onto George's dead forehead, making the sign of the cross with oil. George's skin was cool and very, very smooth, and Sanford and I cried and held on to each other and sang. *"All of us go down to the dust; but even at the grave we make our song, alleluia."* George's body paled and settled as we anointed his forehead with oil and tears and our damp hands.

It was one of those wild Bay Area wintery-spring days, sudden torrential downpours alternating with blasts of shimmery, liquid light; a cold wind blew around the tender new blossoms on the magnolia outside. There was a blur as we dealt with the homely details of death: phoning Paul, who was out of the country, and weeping some more as we broke the news; washing dishes and loading casseroles from the choir into the refrigerator; calling hospice to come fetch the now-irrelevant bottles of medicine lined up on the piano.

But in the room where we sat with George's body there was a steadiness. From time to time Sanford would sob, his breath catching like a stream with a broken branch snagged in its shallows. I kept vigil with my own wet face and runny nose, contemplating tears as what the Book of Revelation calls "waters of life."

Four days later, George's body was converted, fully, to

ash. We held his service at St. Gregory's. It was night, and raining hard, but over a hundred of Sanford's colleagues had showed up to offer their voices. We sang alleluias as we walked together slowly in procession to the altar, laying trembling red tulips down before the urn of ashes and a photo of George smiling, in a tux. It was hard to remember George healthy: the cancer had eaten him so thoroughly in just a few months that the picture seemed to be of a different man.

And then Paul and Sanford and I left the church building, walking out into the night past the baptismal font to the columbarium. We were soaked instantly. Paul, his white and gold robes muddy at the hem, carried the urn on his shoulder, and we pulled open the columbarium's heavy, heavy door and placed George's ashes in one of the small niches honeycombed into the hillside. "You are dust," Paul chanted, "and to dust you shall return."

The rain was so loud it was like thunder battering the night. Water gushed over us from the gutters in great waves as Paul leaned against the door of the columbarium with its mosaic of Jesus, arms outstretched as if levitating out of the tomb. He pushed it shut, and Sanford leaned against me, crying into my wet shoulder.

Some of the congregation had followed us; others

stayed inside the building, singing over and over, faster and faster: "*Christ is risen from the dead, trampling down death by death, and on those in the tombs bestowing life.*" I couldn't tell tears from rain, baptism from burial. There was just the pounding rain sluicing down the drainpipes and pouring over our heads, unable to drown out the singing as we stood there in the dark, outside and inside the church at the same time, weeping and proclaiming the good news.

chapter eleven

For me, living in the Mission is a spiritual practice. It does what I'm too cowardly to do on my own—that is, allow God to be in charge of whatever happens when I walk out my door. The practice means more than being forced to deal with random experiences for no particular reason. Living here in the city of God, I have to consider the strong possibility that God is pointedly, continually, making all things new by deliberately mixing them up.

This is the spiritual principle of *mestizaje*—a word central to the Mission's character that I first heard used when I was a student in Mexico. It means, narrowly, mixed-race, or, less politely, mongrel; but it signifies the larger mixing of cultures and beliefs and practices that is God's gift to Mexico and Mexico's gift to the world. Ancient Mexico, with scores of nations mingling in the multicultural markets of its great cities, was postmodern centuries before modernity even existed. Its powerful religions, like its different Indian and Spanish and African peoples, like its dominated and dominating languages, have long braided into one another, combining and recombining. The struggles of empires, the resistance and defeat and victories of the colonized, the shifting borders of the country keep making things new.

Mestizaje animates the Mission's streets—the actual ones my elderly neighbor Don Miguel sweeps so assiduously, the ones where Rosa Lee's white artist friends hang out. And the blessing of *mestizaje* is embodied by Mexico's patron saint, the Virgin of Guadalupe, who formed my own faith.

Long before she arrived in the New World, the Virgin Mary was at the center of the *mestizo* scandal of Christianity itself: eternal God becoming a mortal human, Spirit mongrelizing irrevocably with flesh to create new life. Mary appeared—and she continues to appear—all over the world, in Poland and Greece and Nigeria and China; pregnant, black-skinned, red-haired, white-robed, crowned, bleeding, sleeping, weeping, rising out of the sea; head bent, hands raised, popping one perfectly round breast into an infant's mouth. She is Dolores,

Mercedes, Soledad, Consuelo, Milagros, Estrella, Luz; our lady of sorrows, mercies, solitude, comfort, miracles, stars, light; or, as Paul simply says, "Herself." Mary is everywhere.

But the Mission's particular devotions are, above all, to Mary the Virgin of Guadalupe. Draped in a blue mantle sprinkled with stars, surrounded by rays of light, she faces the city from every direction. She's painted on the front of the upscale raw-foods vegan restaurant on Mission Street called "Gracias Madre," perhaps the only words in Spanish its earnest owners know besides "guacamole." She's tattooed into the skin of a twenty-five-year-old Salvadoran killer, perhaps the only image of mercy he can accept. She dangles from rearview mirrors and radiates from shopping bags and beach towels. Murals of her adorn at least four different Mission vegetable markets named "Casa Guadalupe"; a pawnshop called "La Virgen" and a bakery named "La Reyna" write her nicknames in script beneath her picture. She's printed on the cheap foil posters and ill-fitting T-shirts and blinking alarm clocks made in China and sold at ghetto dollar stores by Korean shopkeepers who wearily roll up their gates on her feast day, December 12, without knowing who she is or how many different things she means to Mexican moms looking for bargains. She's cast in stone to be plunked down on front steps or in backyards or among the grubby rosebushes by St. Peter's school. She's rendered in glow-in-the-dark plastic and set on a shelf by my front door, so I can put fresh flowers at her feet and light a candle to her before my over-educated Anglo friends show up for dinner.

The story of Guadalupe goes like this. One early December morning in 1531, the Indian peasant and Christian convert Juan Diego is walking past the holy hill of Tepeyac. The brutal occupation of the Spaniards has destroyed the ancient temple there dedicated to the goddess Tonantzin, Mother of Corn and Bringer of Life. Suddenly he's overcome by a vision of a dark-skinned, barefoot, pregnant girl, looking suspiciously like Tonantzin: she's trampling down snakes, bearing codices, crowned with stars. The young woman addresses him in his own Nauhatl language, calling him "my son," and then announces that she is actually Mary, the mother of God, and that he should build a church to her. Frightened and humble, Juan Diego demurs.

"I am a nobody, I am a small rope, a tiny ladder, the tail end, a leaf," he tells her, according to the legend. But the vision insists, so Juan Diego rushes off to share the good news with the Spanish bishop. And the bishop, who is not at all pleased, says, in effect: you stupid Indian, are you crazy? The most Holy Virgin Mary is hardly some heathen brown-skinned girl, have you no respect?

Juan Diego returns to the hilltop with his poncho, prays, and the brilliant vision, who will later be named Guadalupe, appears again. She asks the Indian to open his *tilma,* his cloak, and she fills it with Castilian roses—impossible, sweet-smelling roses in December. He brings it tremulously to the bishop, who falls to his knees when he sees her holy image imprinted on the rough cloth.

Devotions follow; centuries of arguments follow; legends and basilicas follow. Books are filled with conflicting versions of the story. Her name: does it come from the conquerors' Spain, where the Arabic word *wadi*, river, mixed with the Spanish-Latin hybrid word *lupe*, wolf; or does it originate with the Aztecs, where *coatlaxopeuh* means "she who tramples down serpents"? Guadalupe's identity: is she *La Morena, Paloma Blanca*—the dark one, the white dove—or simply *La Reyna*, the Queen of Heaven? Is she syncretized with Tonantzin alone, or also with the pregnant serpent-stomping woman from the Book of Revelation who's clothed with the sun and crowned with twelve stars? And that *tilma*: is it truly incorruptible, or has it been touched up and replaced by fakes? How many times? Is the written Franciscan account or the Nauhatl one or the codex supposedly discovered by the Jesuits more accurate?

And what is going on here, really? Have the stupid, pagan Indians who venerated an Aztec goddess now turned to Our Lady of Guadalupe and finally become real Christians—or has the Mother of God, through *mestizaje*, slyly converted the European Church?

Living in the Mission, I was evangelized by Guadalupe: celebrating her in the streets with others shaped my desire to do more public liturgies, long before we started offering ashes outdoors.

Her feast day takes place in early December, when it's completely dark at four thirty in the morning and the streets seem deserted. There's only an occasional figure to see, bundled against the cold, as I slip out my door and walk through the mist toward the plaza at 24th and Mission, where the procession for Guadalupe will begin. On the corner in front of McDonald's, a small group of

neighbors gathers: older women with scarves and umbrellas and sensible shoes; a Mexican family holding sleepy
toddlers; a serious, jowly Salvadoran man carrying a large
framed print of Herself. A garbage truck drives by, slowly.
There are a dozen, then fifty of us, stamping our feet
to stay warm in the predawn drizzle, and a lady with
a shopping bag bustles around offering everyone little
homemade packets of stale tortilla chips sprinkled with
cinnamon and sugar.

Nobody's really doing much; a few friends are talking
intently, but others just seem to be hanging out, alone
or in twos and threes, waiting for some mysterious signal
so the public liturgy of song and prayer, the *mañanitas,*
can start. At the curb, a tired group of mariachis huddles
together, smoking, their white suits gleaming under the
streetlight. One of them unbuttons his jacket and starts
adjusting a medieval-looking harness that holds his in-
strument, yanking the straps and belts into place wearily;
two other musicians, younger and vainer, kill time showing off to each other with little tooting runs and riffs.
A bus pulls up at the corner and discharges a couple of
nurses on their way to the General Hospital. A car coughs
and heaves in the alley behind the plaza. And suddenly,
with no announcement, right on the dot of five, the violin

player, his hooded eyes unblinking, lifts his bow and saws into a pure high note, and the trumpets join him, and then everyone exhales, and we all start moving east in the dark along 24th Street: *Buenos dias, Paloma Blanca, hoy te vengo a saludar...*

At every corner a few more people appear and fall in step as the hungover mariachis cycle through the same slightly flat, familiar songs. Then an unshaven man with his arms full of roses in plastic wrap, walking with the hood of his sweatshirt pulled up against the rain, starts singing. A lady in a Santa hat joins the procession. Some short, dark Indian guys in windbreakers, talking quietly to each other in Mixtec or Nauhatl, fall in behind grandmothers with gray braids and little boys dressed as Juan Diego with mustaches penciled on their faces. The procession keeps growing.

We're heading to St. Peter's Catholic Church, on 24th Street across from La Palma Mexicatessen. St. Peter's, "serving the Mission since 1878," is the size of a small cathedral, adorned outside with murals depicting heroic indigenous people resisting the conquistadores and modern armies; inside, a gorgeous blue vaulted ceiling, restored after a fire in 1997, soars over ornate stained glass. During the 1980s, St. Peter's helped lead the sanctuary movement for Central American refugees fleeing wars; it remains a center for activism in the Mission. The parish operates an elementary school and a center for immigrants' rights groups, as well as housing and legal aid clinics.

Many of my *vecinos* are members of the parish, but I don't generally go to services there. What moves me about Guadalupe's feast day at St. Peter's is everything that takes place on the edges before the official liturgy begins. Men bring flowers for her with the same obedient, slightly irritated expression they probably wear attending to their own mothers; schoolkids kneel to pray; women cross themselves and gossip, stroll around and light candles. At its borders, St. Peter's liturgy, neither formal nor pious, expresses almost exactly what I love about the Mission itself—where heaven and earth are revealed as part of a continuum, and faith not as a performance but an extension of real life.

The border areas of worship welcome all kinds of strangers. They mix things up. It's striking how much the

street processions for the Virgin of Guadalupe, like our
street Ash Wednesday services, can speak to people who
hold very different beliefs about God and very different
relationships to the Church.

In December 2010 my daughter drove, alone, for
nearly twelve hours to make it in time for the *mañanitas*
at St. Peter's; she'd been working on the border in Arizona, helping friends carry water to immigrants lost in
the desert. Katie is an organizer, emphatically secular, and
knows very little about Christianity, but the figure of
Guadalupe resonates with special meaning for her. Katie
speaks fluent Spanish with a California accent: a Mission
girl who was the only Anglo kid in her second-grade class,
she's a white *mestiza* who doesn't fit into a single identity.

My daughter and I wrapped ourselves in thick scarves
against the chill and headed to 24th Street, through the
changing neighborhood, where familiar barbershops and
dollar stores were being replaced by restaurants with art-
ful, sans-serif menus that leaned heavily on the adjective
"artisan." "*What?*" Katie asked, outraged, when we passed
a newly opened skateboard boutique. "How long has *that*
one been there?"

Tierra Mexicana, tierra Mexicana, the people in the
procession were singing. It was another hymn to Guada-

lupe, hailing her, in rhyming doggerel, as the Protectress of Mexico. "Ha!" said Katie. "Listen." *Attend.*

Katie had sent me a photo of the mural painted on the headquarters of the Arizona activists' group: arms outstretched, the Virgin of Guadalupe held up two plastic jugs of water. It was like the poster by the brilliant Chicana artist Ester Hernandez that showed Guadalupe in mug-shot profile on an FBI "wanted" sign. "WANTED," Hernandez's text read. "Terrorist: *La Virgen de Guadalupe, alias Guadalupe, Reina de las Américas, Virgencita, Nuestra Madre, Tonantzin, Lupe, Lupita*...should be considered powerful and dangerous. For over 160 years, La Virgen de Guadalupe has accompanied countless men, women, and children illegally into the United States...given aid and comfort to unidentified suspects at the time of their death...she has a possibly dangerous light emanating from her body, and is known to have a large, fanatic cult following."

When we got to St. Peter's, Katie linked her arm tightly in mine. "I keep thinking about these guys in the detention center," she said quietly, "and how much they miss their moms." We walked up the stairs and inside, among the crowd.

Whether or not Katie "believes" in the Virgin of

Guadalupe, my daughter's attraction isn't altogether surprising; she grew up surrounded by her presence. But Guadalupe draws people from all over : there's something about the patroness of *mestizaje* that seems to reach not only across cultures, but across doubt.

In 2011, I sent a card to different people I knew, inviting them to join me in the Mission at the *mañanitas*, with a prayer in Spanish and English I'd written: "*Mystical Rose, Mother of the Americas, Prophet of Justice and Star of Mixing It Up: pray for all your children, giving us a burning love and a humble faith, that we may follow your path in the light and grace of your son Jesus.*"

Two friends, Kevin Callahan and Anibal Mejia, said they'd meet me there. Anibal had attended the *mañanitas* before; I suspected, from experience, he'd be late. Kevin, a big, bearded Irish-American math professor, was more likely to make it on time. Kevin was always interested in religious events, though he claimed to reject what he called the "poison" of his Roman Catholic upbringing.

When he got off the BART at 24th and Mission, I could see in the haze of streetlights that Kevin was carrying a homemade statue of the Virgin Mary, a roughly carved chunk of dark wood. "This is Caridad del Cobre," Kevin explained. His devotion was matter-of-fact. "When

Francisco and I went to Cuba to see his family, we got this for you at the shrine where she saved sailors," he explained, showing me a little plastic ship embedded by the Virgin's feet. He handed me the gift. "See?" said Kevin, smiling. "She's just like the one I saw in Knock, in Ireland. I mean, Mary is Mary—she's not geographically positioned. I thought I'd bring this for you since it's Guadalupe's day, and we can get her blessed."

Kevin embraced *mestizaje*: he'd studied Gaelic as well as Hawai'ian; danced hula as well as *cumbia*; and been, at different moments, a member of an African American Catholic church, a Quaker meeting, and a Radical Faerie drum circle. But I'd only recently learned about the time the Virgin of Guadalupe had come to speak directly to him.

Kevin was in his twenties then and living in San Diego, in complete anguish. "My father was in the hospital back in Boston," he recalled. "I was waiting for a blood test that would tell me if I had chronic hepatitis B. I was so afraid, and I was having a meltdown about the Church. I'd tried all these parishes, but I was always on the outside. I knew the priests would just condemn me for being gay." Alone in his room, Kevin decided he needed to get a "divorce" from the Church that rejected him. "You can't excommunicate me," he remembers thinking, defiantly. "I can excommunicate *you*."

But then, in the next moment, as he looked over at a devotional candle printed with a picture of the Virgin of Guadalupe, something his Mexican roommate had picked up at a flea market, the candle spoke to Kevin—in English, just as she had spoken to Juan Diego in Nauhatl—and told him to come visit her in Mexico City. "I'm chattering to myself in my mind all the time," he said, "but this was definitely a real voice, from outside."

Kevin immediately picked up a phone book. He called Aeroméxico and booked a flight, using his high school Spanish. "I asked them if the Virgin of Guadalupe was in Mexico City," he said.

"*Si*," the airline representative said, and so two days later, with no further planning, Kevin stepped off the plane, heaved his backpack onto his shoulders, and figured out how to take the Metro directly to Herself.

The original stone church at Tepeyac was no more, but the new basilica built on its ruins remains one of the largest religious shrines in the world, with a mechanical people-mover carrying millions of pilgrims a year around the vast space, behind the altar and the backdrop with its enormous painting of Guadalupe, past what's claimed to be Juan Diego's original *tilma*. "I got on the conveyor belt," Kevin said. "I really liked the conveyor belt. I went around a few times, and then I went to sit down and look at her."

As Kevin sat in the basilica he began to cry, feeling, he said, "so vulnerable and exposed." This time Guadalupe didn't speak to him in words. "Instead," Kevin said, "there was just this cosmically silent comfort and reassurance coming from her presence all around me. I felt peace, calm, stillness. She wasn't my mother, but she was *the* mother. She was centered, like a mountain of steadiness, and I knew it was okay."

Kevin spent a few more days in Mexico City, hooking up with a sweet gay Mexican architect "who thought it was completely normal that I'd come on a pilgrimage to see Guadalupe," and showed him around the city's ancient Indian sites. He thought a lot about Juan Diego, who'd been dissed by the bishop, gone back to the Virgin for a message that would integrate his tradition with the official one, and turned the Church on its head.

Before he left Mexico, Kevin went back to the basilica, bought two medallions of the Virgin of Guadalupe, and had them blessed at the Mass there. "One was for my father, one for me," he explained. "The intention was that

163

both of us would share the message of peace." When Kevin eventually went home to Boston, he gave the medallion to his father, who wore it around his neck until he died. At that point, "I took it off his body and gave him the one I'd been wearing," Kevin said. "He was buried with mine."

"It's a long story," said Kevin. He looked at his watch. We ducked past a storefront draped in erratically blinking Christmas lights; I could see their reflection on the wet, slick sidewalk. "I've got to leave you in a minute and catch the BART to work."

"I know I brought the wrong Virgin for you today," Kevin said, looking down at the Cuban statue in my arms, "and I'm this tall white guy." He smiled at a little Mexican girl who stood next to us wearing a Hello Kitty sweatshirt. "But I know I belong here."

Anibal arrived at the celebration a little later, after Kevin left for work, and managed to find me in the crowd. He looked rumpled, and his face was icy when we kissed. "Damn!" Anibal said, shivering. "It's so cold. Where's the ladies with the *atole*?"

"Up at St. Peter's," I said. Women from the parish always prepared steaming vats of *atole* and hot chocolate for the *mañanitas*, and offered the drinks with *pan dulce* to worshippers at the entrance of the church. Anibal chained his bike to a lamppost, I stuck the statue of Mary under my arm, and we continued walking along behind the mariachis, talking.

Anibal was another *mestizo* believer. I'd met him through the food pantry at St. Gregory's: he was a clinical case manager for homeless, mentally ill drug users, including several I knew, and worked on one of the worst blocks of the Mission. He attended services at St. Gregory's from time to time, and I learned that he was a priest in the Candomblé tradition, serving its *orixas*, or spirits. He invited me to participate with his congregation in the house liturgies he led. "We love Jesus, too," Anibal reassured me, "and, of course, his mom."

"Knowledge of Orixa is cumulative," Anibal wrote, trying to explain how the pieces of his faith came together. "You get initiated or somehow come into the religion and you just start hearing a story here or there, learning a ritual, absorbing the habits and conventions of the practice, connecting the dots between all these things, then, as life happens, you realize that the rituals, rules, and stories are actually telling something even more profound, something about you and life, and it keeps stacking up, more stories, more meanings, and on and on…"

Anibal had a Honduran dad, a white American mom, and an ancient, stern Brazilian priestess, Iyá Marinete Martins de Souza, as his godmother. Initiated in Brazil into a syncretic tradition that mixed Yoruban practices with Christian myths, Old World and New World deities, Anibal returned to reveal and express Candomblé in the contemporary context of the Mission.

His own flock looked as *mestizo* as the city: gay and straight, Latino and white, black and Cuban and Chinese-Filipino. Mostly young but with a few elders and a couple of babies, they tended to be deeply reverent, although not dogmatic. "We're all mixed up," I heard Anibal preach once, the smoke from *copal* encircling his close-cropped hair. Anibal had no interest in creating historical reenactments of nostalgic, supposedly pure liturgies imported from Brazil, "recited in pristine orthodoxy, kept safe by taboos." Instead, he wanted to queer the religion, mix a bit of *nam pla* into the traditional rice and beans, belt out "I'll Fly Away" after the *congeros* chanted in Portuguese.

Once, following a late-night ceremonial cleansing with a bottle of Florida water passed from hand to hand, I even saw one of Anibal's Candomblé deacons pick up a rosary. "*Hail Mary*," he proclaimed, his slender body bent forward, "*full of Grace, the Lord is with you*." We chanted the rosary together, over and over, and when we were done, we recited the Lord's Prayer, and finally sang the most traditional Christian hymn imaginable, "How Great Thou Art." When I told Paul about this liturgy later, he laughed in astonishment. "That is just the most perverse thing I've ever heard," he said admiringly.

Anibal and I passed La Reyna Bakery, which, like all Mexican bakeries, always smelled deceptively delicious. It had taken me forever to stop getting suckered by the fragrance of yeast and orange and anis that wafted all day from bakeries in the Mission, where, inevitably, the pastries tasted of nothing but over-sweetened tissue paper. This morning the owners had hauled a wooden table out in front of a mural of Guadalupe, Queen of Heaven, which gave the shop its name, and set out buckets of fresh red roses to honor her. Inside the bakery, an early crew was pulling trays of fresh bread out of a wall of ovens.

Anibal crossed himself. "She's everywhere," he said.

We arrived at St. Peter's, and I paused at the portico as the crowd swept past us. Partly it was the allure of the warm chocolate on the tables below, sending out clouds of steam through the chilly air; partly, though, it was my long-standing hesitation about Church. It was more comfortable to be watching from the half-dark than participating inside the busy, bright building. "I kind of want to stay outdoors," I said. "I always like it better."

Anibal looked at me quizzically. I'd been trying to explain my struggles with the Church to him, ever since he'd named me in front of his congregation as "a priest of Jesus," echoing Paul's comment, and urged me to take responsibility for evangelizing. Priesthood, according to Anibal, wasn't just "spiritual case management," like the work we shared with crazy junkies and parishioners, but was more like what Mark called "making God's presence real to others." That meant, Anibal suggested, resisting the seductive lure of feeling separate from other people, and from the Church.

"I just don't want to hear that same boring sermon they do here every year," I said defensively, shifting the statue in my arms. "Let's go get some breakfast." And turning my back on the faithful, who were streaming up the stairs of St. Peter's, I walked with Anibal to a café on the corner. Where, like everywhere else that morning, a picture of Guadalupe, wreathed in roses, beckoned.

A week later, Anibal sent me a long meditation wrapping together the Christian stories of the Annunciation and Visitation and Mary's Magnificat with the Candomblé story of the spotted guinea hen, totem animal of the priesthood. His essay began and ended with Guadalupe, and our conversation in the Mission.

"We were there," he wrote, "but part of us seemed unpresent, observing as outsiders, marginal like anthropologists or tourists. If we feel marginal, if we find ourselves standing outside the Church yet on its steps, giggling at its obtuseness and obstinacy, feeling righteous yet disempowered, privileged yet weirdo; if we feel 'other' because of our priesthood, we shouldn't stay long in that lone place. If we stay there in the cast-out parts of the world and ourselves, not quite in the Church nor out of it, without opening fully to the communion of the Spirit, we become lone wolves with nothing but hungry eyes for our flock.

"Guadalupe is *mestiza*, mixed, an outsider to pure races, to the pedigreed, the washed, the saved... pregnant with the Coming of God, quenching thirst. Let her guide us to water."

And so I did. Months after that wintry morning, on Ash Wednesday, 2012, I'd find myself on 24th Street again, praying in another public liturgy in the Mission, communing with another odd assortment of companions and drinking in the blessing.

chapter twelve

There are times in the Mission, toward the end of an afternoon, when light slides at a slant through the city's air, illuminating each face with an almost holy glow. White people seem golden; black people gleam; and brown faces, from that of the scruffiest wino in a baseball cap to the fussiest baby yelling in its stroller, are radiant. The stout Salvadoran woman selling her unlikely combination of CDs and shellfish from a blanket on the sidewalk has the skin of a luminescent Madonna, and deep violet shadows give a Dutch-master profundity to the illustration of a head with flowing tresses painted on the chipped window of Ana's Belleza & Nails.

At first I couldn't see it. All I could focus on, crouching on the sidewalk, was getting the plastic wrap off our little jars of ashes without spilling them. My cassock was already grubby where I'd wiped my hands, and nobody else had thought to bring extra paper towels. "Hey, Sara," I heard Bertie say, "isn't that our friend?"

Wisdom, attend. I looked up. The air was breathing and shining around us, and a short older man in a pressed white shirt was heading straight toward the card-table altar, beaming at Bertie. "I think it's the dude who goes to St. Peter's," Bertie said to me as I stood up. "The one who offered to pray for us last year."

I remembered him: not only had the man offered to pray for us, fervently, but he'd pressed his business card on me, "in case Father or you ever need some new clothes." His store, all the way at the end of Mission Street in Daly City, was called Fashion for the New Millennia Look; to my great regret, I hadn't ever managed to stop by.

But I got to my feet and we all greeted each other a little shyly; now I could fully see the brightness around the man, our group of Ash Wednesday volunteers, and the entire crummy plaza. It was like the Transfiguration, if the holy mountain had MUNI buses.

Vik, looking very Midwestern and blond, was on his knees busily spooning *copal* onto the coals in the rusted iron thuribles; he'd recruited a couple of other church nerds from the seminary he attended, and they were all

171

busily working together. Behind them, a burly deacon in a clerical collar and a woman I knew from Holy Innocents' food pantry were securing the FORGIVE MORE poster to the cast-iron fence. I thought I recognized an activist who worked alongside Mark's lover Cris at the Housing Committee. A gray-bearded priest wearing a brightly colored stole whose single-syllable Anglo name I could never remember—Bob? Ted? Fred?—smiled kindly at me, unpacked the jars of ashes, and started handing them out.

I saw him approach Kelsey, who generally managed an excellent poker face that allowed her to seem simply like a pleasant middle-aged white lady. It was only recently I'd heard Kelsey talk openly about her unsettling desire for more God.

"I'm finding the things that mean the most to me in Christianity have to do with the body," she said. "The singing: if singing wasn't there, I wouldn't be in church. Bread and wine. It carries you along. What you do with your body is something you can lean into, even if you're not believing that much on any particular day."

When I let Kelsey know about our plans for Ash Wednesday in the Mission, she volunteered at once. "I want to have experiences," she declared, "and at this point, the messier the better. I want to have more life."

"Like Jesus promises?" I asked. "Life, abundant?"

"Exactly!" Kelsey said. "Yes. I've been someone who can stand back and observe on the side of the river...and now I want to wade in."

"I know what you mean," I told Kelsey.

So now Kelsey, wearing a black cassock, was in the river. She was holding the little jar of ashes, talking gently to Vera, who was standing next to her in street clothes.

I looked at Vera, realizing how wrenching the decision to move to San Francisco after her sister's suicide must have been. Despite the continuing love and support of her community in Texas, Vera felt it would be a "betrayal" to stay the same, as if nothing had happened. She had to convert, begin again. Moving away from her family and friends, even changing her relationship with the Church, seemed necessary, Vera said, as "a testament to how Audrey's life and death shape me." Today, on the anniversary of her sister's death, she'd done the inverse of Kelsey's action: she'd come to the Mission not to wade into the river, but simply to witness.

"I've felt safest on the periphery," Vera explained quietly. I knew exactly what she meant, too. We kissed, and she took a step back.

A flock of pigeons was circling around the plaza as we

173

began to pair up, one person with ashes and one carrying a smoking thurible. There was a faint rumbling underneath our feet as a train pulled away from the BART station, and commuters began to emerge from the escalator into the intensifying golden light.

"Beautiful," I told Bertie, whose own face was glowing.

And then, just like that, we were off. It felt like the moment at the beginning of the Palm Sunday service each year when I remove my wristwatch, put it away until after Easter, and plunge untethered into God's time. Singing, praying, eating, weeping, I enter the current of Holy Week with my whole Church to swim in *kairos* time, out of control.

I remembered what a friend pointed out the first year we offered ashes in the street. "Whenever you touch someone with the ashes," she said, "it's like time stops. It just *stops*, over and over."

Bertie was waiting in front of me. He bowed his head wordlessly. I looked at him, surprised by more tenderness than I'd ever imagined, and stuck my thumb into the little glass container.

"Bertie," I whispered. I traced an irregular line of ashes onto his pale, young forehead. Already my fingernails were dirty, and already I didn't care. I was undone. "Bertie. You. Ah. Remember you are dust, and to dust you shall return."

"Amen," Bertie said. He stayed there, bent over, for a moment, his breath like the decay of a long note of music. Then he straightened. He took the container from me. I bowed.

"Remember you are dust," Bertie pronounced with exquisite clarity, pressing the ashes into my skin. "And to dust you shall return."

Our little group seemed to separate into two: those used to serving inside churches, who wanted to remain by the altar waiting for people to come to them, and the more free-range Christians who couldn't wait to peel out.

I couldn't wait. I couldn't stand still. I looked at Kelsey, her forehead newly smudged, and at Vera, shy in her denim jacket, smiling at us, and nodded. "Good to go?" I asked them.

Kelsey took a thurible, and Vik carefully loaded it up with a fresh charcoal and a heaping, dusty spoonful of incense. "Good to go," she said brightly.

"Let's walk up Mission first," I said. "A lot of people have been working all day; let's see if anyone wants ashes."

Bertie made a V with his fingers and waved at the three of us. "Peace," he said. "See you soon."

Before we even got out of the plaza, though, we came across a leathery woman in a blue windbreaker slumped against the wall, licking a vanilla ice cream cone with the dreamy inattentiveness of a regular heroin user, as if she might, at any moment, forget to swallow. But when we crossed into her field of vision she waved the cone, beckoning us over, and turned up her face for the ashes.

"*Recuerda que eres polvo*," I said, "*y al polvo volverás*." Vera swallowed, hard.

I stopped for a young black bike messenger, who hailed us and lifted his face dutifully. A chubby sixteen-year-old girl, heading toward the escalator to the train with her friend, looked over her shoulder, trying to figure out how much more pathetic we were than any other adults, and if we were dangerous.

"What's up with *that?*" she challenged Kelsey as I crossed the messenger's forehead. "Thanks," the boy said, and wove off. I turned toward the girls.

"Ash Wednesday," Kelsey said. "You want some ashes?"

"Uh, what for?" asked the girl. *You are so stupid*, the

tone of her voice implied. *You must be kidding.* But she didn't move away. Her friend tugged at her elbow. "You know, like church," she said, pulling the girl closer. "Come on, get some."

"You first," said the chubby girl, and so I quickly crossed her friend's forehead and heard her say, a little grudgingly, "Amen."

"Let's try some stores," I said.

At the first taqueria we entered, the one that served the Mission's most delicious, greasy, spicy, salty *al pastor* tacos, the counterman put down his knife as soon as he saw us. "Hi!" he said, "thank you for coming!" I gave ashes to him, to a silent, sad-faced guy chopping up *carne asada* in a funk, and to a cheerful woman in charge of the cash register. The counterman offered us a drink of melon *agua fresca* and then directed me to the back storeroom, where two other workers were unloading boxes. They looked unsurprised to see us and both crossed themselves before dipping their heads down to receive the ashes, the blessing. "Thank you," the workers said.

Good, I thought. At least nobody's offended yet. As we left the storeroom, Kelsey's thurible clanking, I tried not to catch the attention of an unkempt customer sitting near the door staring at us in a hostile way. But then I

177

paused, looking at him as directly as I dared. "Would you like ashes?" I asked. The man ignored me. "Come on," urged Vera, opening the door. "There's someone on the sidewalk waiting for you."

The sidewalk was teeming: moms with babies in strollers, girls in tight jeans talking on their phones as they bounced along, shopkeepers darting out to steady their teetering displays of yucca and oranges. People flowed past like the river in Psalm 46 that "delights the city of God." A Middle Eastern man scooped up his toddler and gave the boy a noisy kiss, and another line from a Psalm popped into my mind: "Blessed be God, who has shown me the wonders of his love in a besieged city."

"He'd like some ashes, please," said the man, lifting the boy high as he squirmed and giggled. "Hold still, it's not going to hurt."

I crossed the boy's forehead and then the father's, then turned to the short, silent older Mexican woman who was standing patiently behind them, as if waiting in line. "Would you like ashes?" I asked. She nodded, and I dipped a thumb again in the jar. I didn't tell her it wouldn't hurt.

"Amen," she said.

We walked on. At the Mission Cultural Center, a neighborhood arts studio, a couple of Chicano hipsters wearing trendy eyeglasses and sneakers waved us inside; at the florist next door, an exhausted-looking grandmother smiled but remained seated among buckets of roses, stripping off the leaves as she received the ashes. I didn't even glance into the doorway of the next business, a brightly-lit evangelical bookstore conspicuously missing any images of the Virgin of Guadalupe. "No thank you," an upright woman there had told me icily the previous year. "We're Christians."

Another restaurant, a Chinese bakery, a quasi-gentrified bar. A kid on a bike, a kid on a skateboard, a man in a wheelchair. You are dust. Amen. To dust you'll return. Amen.

Amen, amen, amen.

I trotted past a guy selling bacon-wrapped hot dogs, with their delicious burnt-onion smell, and paused to give him ashes. I was blessing an older Filipina lady pushing a shopping cart when a big Chicano man pulled up in a red truck, turned on his blinkers, and threw open the door. "Oh! Can I have those?" he called out. "Wait, my mom is in the backseat—can you come give her some, too?" It felt intoxicating, wild, urgent. "Let's keep going another few blocks," I said to Kelsey and Vera. "We could try the library, and McDonald's."

Around the corner, the middle-aged clerk at the library checkout desk beckoned us closer. Her hair was clipped back, and she looked tired. She said softly, "I saw your sign that said 'forgive more.' That's what I need in my life right now. I need to forgive more."

We gave ashes to her and to a few nerdy schoolkids, and started walking back toward the plaza.

"I'm glad to be here," Vera said suddenly.

"Me, too," said Kelsey.

Kelsey had tried to explain her desire to be part of Ash Wednesday on the street. "I need to be with people who aren't like me," she said. "I just want—I don't know, I want to feel connected to them in another way, let my little chatting judging evaluating mind quiet down and just *be* with other human beings."

That's exactly what people in the Mission had done for me. So many strangers and neighbors and friends had nodded hello, offered food, looked at me, walked alongside me, touched me, even, like the bearded gnome-lady, given me spiritual advice and a fresh lemon. They had just *been* with me. They had blessed me.

"Hey! Over here!" A tall, exceptionally animated guy in a blue jacket spotted us and was waving excitedly. "Hey," he said in rapid-fire Spanish, grabbing my arm, "come with me! Around the corner! I've got these friends! In the beauty salon! Two beauty salons!"

I followed as he loped ahead, nearly running. "They work so much!" he shouted. "Guatemalans, just like me! We work hard! Nine, ten, twelve hours, and by the time you're done the church is closed! But you still need ashes! Come on!"

I lost Kelsey and Vera as the man turned quickly onto 23rd Street. I'd never been in this beauty salon, with its gold-flecked wallpaper, though I passed it almost every day. In the old days it had been a movement bookstore and a meeting place for the Socialist Workers Party, and earnest murals of heroic revolutionaries still adorned its façade: a somewhat faded portrait of Nelson Mandela looked down on the hand-lettered sign that now advertised eight-dollar haircuts and highlights, semi-permanent, for forty bucks.

The man flung the door open and proudly waved me in. "Look what I brought you!" he exclaimed to the hairdressers and their clients as everyone looked up, slightly surprised, mid-coif. "I brought you the cross!"

"Oh, okay," said one hairdresser, a heavy woman laced into a flowered smock. "Oh, it must be Ash Wednesday!" She put down her scissors and came over to me. "Please," she said.

All the women nodded. "I brought you the Church!" the man said to them, happily.

"Thanks," said another hairdresser. "Amen." She lifted her client's foil-wrapped bangs off her forehead and motioned to me. One at a time, I gave ashes to all the women seated in the chairs, while the receptionist dialed a friend on her cell phone. "Hey," she said, "it's Ash Wednesday, do you want the sister to come to your shop?"

But I was out the door already, urged along by the Guatemalan man. "Next one! They need ashes! Let's go!"

Beside the old movement bookstore was a *santeria* store, with its powders and candles and devotional altars to the *orixas*, and two doors down there was yet another beauty salon. It was hard to see how anyone could possibly make money cutting hair, given the utter saturation of the market, but somehow new salons, with almost identical designs, kept opening in the Mission. On the sidewalk, the smell of industrial-perm ammonia mingled with *copal* smoke wafting from the *santeria* store. The Guatemalan man held the door open for me and pressed his business card into my hand, grinning wildly. "God bless you! Call me if you need anything! Anything!"

"*Recuerdas que eres polvo*," I kept saying to strangers, "*y al polvo volverás.*"

I said the words to a very shy woman, who kept her eyes tightly shut as she received the ashes, and to a bored-looking *paletero* standing by his ice cream cart. I was saying "*Recuerdas que eres polvo*" again to the first of a trio of middle school kids in parochial-school uniforms, when someone walking by finished for me: "...*y al polvo te conviertas.*"

You'll *turn* into dust? Or you'll *return* to dust? Had I been using the wrong verb all afternoon?

But as the last plaid-skirted girl skipped off, smudged, I realized I'd lost my shame about my messed-up Spanish or my messed-up, sooty hands. Being on the street opened a space that was, mercifully, less about liturgical performance and more about devotion; less about my pride and perfectionism than about the shared experience of God. This wasn't the half-in, half-out feeling I'd suffered standing with Anibal on the threshold of St. Peter's; nor was it a private spiritual epiphany. I was just *there*. And in each moment of encounter—brief, intense, unpredictable—God's presence flared out, as if my hand and a stranger's face became, together, the tent of meeting.

I found Vera and Kelsey back on the south side of 24th and Mission, deep in discussion. A worried-looking white woman had stopped them and presented her little girl.

"I don't deserve it," she said, "but at least give her the ashes, she hasn't done anything wrong."

"They're for everyone," Kelsey said. "You don't have to deserve them."

And as Kelsey bent down to touch the child, a couple of other women joined the conversation, offering their own opinions.

"It's for forgiveness," said one, her arms full of grocery bags. "Like, you tell God the things you've done bad, he forgives you, then you get the ashes to remind you."

A younger woman looked doubtful. "But you have to take communion first. Or you can't get ashes."

The mother looked at each of them, and at Kelsey and Vera. "Well," the woman said, "could I just have a blessing?"

A Latino teenager slowed, doing a slight double-take as he took in the scene. Then he swept off his baseball cap with a grand gesture and grinned at me. "Hey, hook me up, too!" he called.

We walked on.

"I don't even know what *this* is," said Kelsey, "but I could do this forever."

The city of God, says the Book of Revelation, is like a bride adorned and made ready for her husband, coming down out of heaven. We stopped for refills at the plaza. Vik was still there, and as I put more ashes into my jar he told me about the man who got off the bus and wanted to make a full confession. "On his *knees*," said Vik, sounding scandalized. It didn't sound that odd to me; perhaps my religious-nut radar was becoming hopelessly jammed, but wanting to confess on Ash Wednesday seemed pretty reasonable. I wished I'd done it more myself.

A kid, maybe nineteen, who'd been hanging with the group of guys drinking and smoking at the corner of the plaza, came over tentatively. He was thin, with dark hair, and his baggy T-shirt made him look like a child dressed in his father's clothes. He stood next to me and gestured over toward a messy pile of religious votive candles, helium balloons, and empty rum bottles the drinkers had heaped around a lamppost.

"That's our friend," he said. "What happened?" I asked, taking in the signifying junk. "He died," the teenager said flatly. "He just died. His heart stopped. Can I have some ashes?"

I rubbed ashes into his forehead, his fragile, human forehead.

"Thanks," the kid said.

"I'm sorry about your friend," I said. "What was his name?"

"David," said the kid. "Same as me."

"David," I exclaimed. "That's my brother's name, too. I'll pray for your friend, and my brother, and you."

The teenager paused. "Also, another thing?" he said. He looked at me a little hesitantly. "When I was incarcerated, I read the Bible. There was this dude in it named David, same as us. He was a king."

Kings, murderers, dead men, gangbangers, little brothers: we're dust, and to dust we shall return.

It still felt strange sometimes to be out on the streets of the Mission and not bump into all the people I knew were gone for good; once in a while I'd still expect to see a friend who'd actually been dead for decades. Now, carrying ashes around the city, I thought about the era when so many men I loved were dying and nobody knew what to do with ashes.

For a few of the dead, there might have been services at a cemetery or columbarium, often uncomfortable occasions with clergy trying hard not to use the word "AIDS." For those with a sense of humor or drama, there might have been quirky celebrations: one guy I knew put his best friend's ashes, "for revenge," in a bright yellow smiley-face cookie jar; some ACT-UP activists dumped ashes in front of the White House. For most of us, there were just awkward deliveries of surprisingly heavy boxes that wound up, unopened, on a closet shelf—you couldn't really throw the ashes out, but were

you supposed to lug them around from rental apartment to rental apartment for the rest of your life?—or
in illegal outdoor scatterings at vaguely "spiritual" loca-
tions.

I'd carried one friend's ashes from the Mission out
to Land's End, where sweet alyssum was blooming on
the cliffside and the Pacific crashed and broke below our
group of mourners. His mother was there, crying, and
half a dozen friends, two of them very sick themselves.
We didn't say anything aloud. I reached into the container
when it was my turn and tossed a handful into the sky.
When the ashes blew back into my open mouth, they
tasted slightly of salt and dust.

My chaplain friend Will had survived those days and
told me about an Ash Wednesday back then on the streets
with a friend. "We were walking to the gay neighborhood
after getting ashes," Will said. "This was before I got really
sick myself. It was a bad time: every week you'd pick up
the paper and see who else had died.

"It was so powerful to see the marks of the ashes on
each other's faces," Will said softly, "and to notice all the
men around us who had marks from Kaposi's sarcoma on
their faces—I mean, every fourth or fifth guy would have
KS lesions. I felt this deep, deep affinity with my friend,

and all the strangers with AIDS. Like being on the verge of dying was the depth of our life together."

It was getting darker. Dianda's, the old-school Italian bakery that sold hot cross buns every Lent, was still open; Mission families, as they had for generations, were standing in line for almond cakes and cannolis and little dry cookies with glacé cherries in them. The first year we offered ashes in the street, one of the bakers, a large woman in an apron, had turned around with a three-layer frosted birthday cake in her hands, leaning carefully over the cake so I could mark her forehead. Today, a different woman paused as she rang up a purchase and bent toward me, giving off the smell of vanilla, and I could see a long ragged scar snaking down her neck.

How many people had received ashes from us today— two hundred? Four hundred? At the taqueria next door, a man working the griddle fetched all the prep cooks, calling them by name to come and receive ashes, and customers beckoned us over to their tables, spread with plates of tacos and foil-wrapped burritos. "It's her first time," a light-skinned black woman with braids explained to me, urging her daughter forward. I thought about Rosa Lee trying to explain what she'd seen happening to adults at Holy Innocents when their children received ashes. "Baptism's pretty," she'd said, "there's the little white dress, the godparents, if you don't listen too carefully to the words it's a nice ceremony. But when you put ashes on their baby it's different. They realize, hey, God's in control of this kid, not me."

Then we were at McDonald's, our last stop before we finished up, and we pushed open the smudged glass doors to the noisy, crowded dining room. I gave ashes to families eating French fries, to a woman who never stopped talking on her cell phone, to the antsy security guard, and to some gangbangers eyeing the security guard.

Kelsey and Vera stood with me in front of a booth with a group of rowdy high school kids who were poking one another as they watched us offer ashes, daring each other to go first. One girl kept saying, "Oh, I'm scared, what's it gonna do to me? Okay, I'm ready, no, I'm scared. No, I want it." I waited, the jar of ashes in my hand. It was noisy all around us, but I realized I was praying. Finally, she just turned her face up and said, "Do it."

We were on our way out when a small, serious Mayan

woman, sitting alone at a greasy table, unwrapped her tiny baby from an acrylic blanket and held him up to me. "He's one and one half weeks old," she said proudly. I crossed his forehead with ashes, took a deep breath, and told the baby he was going to die.

And then his mother, like everyone else we'd met that afternoon, said *thank you.*

Why would you say *thank you* when a stranger tells you that you're going to die?

Because the truth is a blessing.

"It's just true," Vera had said of her sister's death. "This true thing has happened, and so you have to change."

chapter thirteen

I t was nearly six thirty, time to go back for the last service at St. Gregory's. I hated to stop. On the plaza,
Bertie and his parishioners rolled up their posters, kissed
us good-bye, and left for Holy Innocents, where Bertie
was going to lead an evening service inside the building.
Vik and his friends wiped off their hands, kissed us, and
got back on the BART, to return to their seminary. "I'll
talk to you soon," Vera said, and kissed me quickly before
she slipped away. Kelsey helped carry all the gear back to
the side street where I'd parked, kissed me, and said good-
bye; she was on her way to sing with the choir for the final
Ash Wednesday service at Grace Cathedral. I leaned on
my car, unbuttoning the dusty cassock, my face covered
in kisses and ash, alive in the holy city.

The air felt cool on my arm as I drove with my window

rolled down through the Mission. Past the open door of the Mexicatessen, with its smells of meat and lime and corn; past the busy steps of St. Peter's and the playground where a few kids were still clinging to the monkey bars; past the General Hospital, where I slowed, half-hoping and failing to see Mr. Claws among the patients smoking in their wheelchairs by the entrance. Past Walgreens and the biker bar and the Vietnamese sandwich shop, and up over the darkening hill to St. Gregory's.

I opened the door quietly and took a seat among the twenty or so worshippers gathered inside the church. Mark wasn't there—I hoped he was finally home with Cris instead of still stuck at his office job. Sanford was in the cantor's chair and Paul was presiding, his powerful voice wrapping around the notes of the opening prayer. *"Grant us, most merciful God, the lamp of charity which never fails, that it may burn in us and shed its light on those around us, and that by its brightness we may have a vision of that holy City, where dwells the true and never-failing light, Jesus Christ our Lord..."*

This evening Ash Wednesday service was one of my favorite liturgies of the year, when, lighting oil lamps, we slowly chanted verses from the prophet Isaiah. The text promised a new Jerusalem raised from ruins, where the people of God would dwell forever. Candles flickered, illuminating the gold-leaf halos of the icons we'd set out that morning, and blue ribbons of incense rose toward heaven. And when it came time to kneel all I could think was, "This place is so small."

Church *is* small. Church is so much more cowardly and less imaginative than it has to be; it's so mindlessly stubborn about its own correctness, proud of its own power, petty, judgmental, and unkind toward those who disagree. But these failures of the institution, as the experiences of Ash Wednesday reveal, are precisely the same as my own. My nostalgia, my desire to stay indoors, to refuse new experiences, to ignore demanding neighbors, to hide from the Spirit in the habitual—these are the sins that call for repentance.

Because though incarnation is at the center of Christian faith, it can be scary to experience it as we say in my neighborhood, *en su propia carne*, in your own meat, here and now. It feels way too dangerous to mix up the grungy facts of our bodies—blood, sex, breath, illness, dirt, death—with the Spirit, which most of us would prefer to imagine as elevated and immaterial. Bodies aren't stable: they're vulnerable. And when random bodies slam into each other unplanned, the way they do in the streets of a *mestizo* city, anything can happen. Sometimes it can feel safer to worship indoors, in a temple of stone, where the company is more predictable. Where the fire will seem smaller and the overshadowing cloud less dark and the holy ground more neatly fenced in.

But a spiritual life *is* a physical life, shared with other people. Those who hunger. Who thirst. Who sing. Who are born to teenage girls on the wrong side of town and die as criminals; who eat with their hands and yell at their friends; who spit and kiss and groan in labor; who bleed and stumble and drink cool water; who breathe on one another and create, out of these crudest physical facts, a mystical body.

Church *is* small. But the good news is that any temple made by human hands must always be too small to hold God. And so the rowdy, heterodox Church of God's whole bickering body is set loose in the creation God made to praise him, set loose in the incarnate meat of Jesus, set loose all over the world. "The world," says Gerard Manley Hopkins, "is charged with the grandeur of God...it will flame out like shining from shook foil."

God's love for us is as excessive as rain falling forever on the ocean. And the entire outpouring of words and gestures, stories and songs, and objects we offer in response keeps flooding forth, pooling, eddying, and recombining over centuries like the river of life, haunting each hidden corner, flowing to sanctify every niche of every place we recognize as the city of God. Like the one glimpsed on Don Miguel's steps, in St. Gregory's entryway, or above the cash register in a Mission grocery store, where a beckoning-cat statue and a postcard of Mary are set on top of the soft-drink cooler, on a bed of red shook foil.

Inside and outside of church buildings, on Ash Wednesday and every other day, the people of God keep talking with God. We saturate our cities with worship, in eager imitation of God's saturating holiness. We mix up remembered prayers and misremembered rituals, calling on ancestors and accidentally encountered strangers whose own conflicted conversations with God leak into us. We kneel, we cover our heads, we cross ourselves, we invent more ways to kiss, kiss, kiss. We shout hosanna, hallelujah; we say sister, brother, mother, father; we sneeze and say God bless you; we curse and speak in tongues. And because voice and gestures are never enough, we pile on things: rosaries, roses, petals, pennies on a dead man's eyes, amulets, icons, books, bread, wine, water, milk, honey, oil, salt, fire, ashes, more. More. Mix it all up. More.

The sages of the Talmud suggest at least a hundred occasions each day, of tragedy as well as beauty, to offer benediction. Waking up, seeing a deformed person, moving the bowels, hearing of the death of a friend, eating fruit: these are opportunities to bless God. The *Manual for Priests*, published first in 1944 by the Episcopal monks of the Society of St. John the Evangelist and revised in 1978, offers its prayers and blessings in the same spirit, in order to "bear witness to the sovereignty of God: that he rules over the whole of life from birth to death, and that no concern of his children can be unimportant in his sight; there is no area of life from which God is shut out."

In the *Manual*'s astonishing index there are blessings for cattle and herds, for pregnant women, for eggs at Easter, for machinery, for monstrances, for space crafts, and, filed under "A," for "Anything Whatsoever." That one, the key one, reads: "*O God by whose Word all things are sanctified, pour thy blessing upon this___ and grant that whosoever shall use it with thanksgiving may, by the invocation of thy holy Name, receive from thee, who art its maker, health of body and protection of soul, through Christ our Lord, Amen."*

After the blessing is given, the Anything Whatsoever is then sprinkled with holy water, "to the center, then to the left, lastly to the right." Notes the *Manual*, sternly: "Blessings ought always to be given in the proper form."

But there is no area of life from which God is shut out, and the "proper form" can't be contained in a manual, limited to the actions of official priests, or contained in a service inside a sanctuary. The blessing, as my neighbors and my neighborhood keep showing me, has been set loose: God has left the building.

Martha wasn't home when I finally trudged up our steps carrying one last milk crate full of ashes and incense that I'd forgotten to take out of the car trunk and leave at St. Gregory's. I kicked off my shoes in the entryway, under the shelf that held the glow-in-the-dark Guadalupe statue. For years, I'd displayed a red hammer-and-sickle poster from the South African Communist Party in that same spot; now the movement relic was in my office, evoking the same mix of irony and devotion I felt for the schlocky religious statue.

Wow, my feet were really tired.

I switched on the kitchen light. There was a long note on the counter. "Honey," Martha had written on a scrap of lined paper, "I knew you'd been up to no good when that little girl next door came by with her deaf mom, asking for ashes for them and Tia Linda. I told them you'd stop by when you got back from church. I'm at the gym. See you soon."

Busted, busted.

At least I can do this last one in normal clothes, I thought, imagining how I'd joke with Mark and Bertie about the final straw of this long, tiring day. But then I caught myself smiling. That crying baby next door, the one who'd kept us awake with her distress, had become a person who rang our doorbell boldly, who could translate her mother's signed request for ashes. I didn't really want Ash Wednesday to end. I wanted to see my neighbors.

The strange thing about repentance is how a new heart can show up, un-willed, as if a change has been worked under the surface of consciousness, completely apart from effort or explicit choice. As convoluted and impure as my desires might be, as lazy and self-absorbed and fussy as I acted, something was changing me, bringing me closer to what I'd prayed for.

I put on my shoes again, grabbed my keys and a jar of ashes and went next door. There was a little lamp in Don Miguel's window, behind the faded curtains. Years ago, Doña Luz used to sit by that window all the time, casting her suspicious gaze on the street, keeping an eye on her family, the neighbors, the double-parkers, trash-tossers, and pot-smokers. She loved this city, I realized.

At the top of their steps, I rang the bell and a tousled teenaged boy appeared behind the gate. I held up the jar. "Linda asked could I bring ashes?"

He opened the door immediately, as if he recognized me. "Oh, yeah, come on in!" the boy said. "She's not here, but come in; could me and my girlfriend get some?"

I hadn't expected this welcome. I followed him down the hallway, past the dim, crowded living room with its tweed recliners and family photos and houseplants, and into the kitchen, full of cooking smells, where a girl stood at the sink, rinsing off some dishes. I didn't know what to say.

"Thank you for coming," said the girl, turning toward me. She had an angel's skin, with dark eyebrows, and she was barefoot, wearing a wrinkled T-shirt.

I drew the ashes carefully across their foreheads. The boy smiled shyly.

"Would it be okay," he asked me, "I mean, if you have extra, could you maybe leave a little bit for the others when they get back later?"

There was a pile of paper goods on the kitchen table, and I pointed at the stack. "Give me a plate?" A little shakily, I poured some ashes into the smallest paper plate and then handed it to the boy, swallowing hard. "Here. You know what to say to everyone, right?"

"You're dust and to dust you will return," he said.

I made the sign of the cross between us and said, "Just put your thumb in the ashes and do this on their forehead when you say the blessing. Thank you so much."

"You're welcome," the boy said. The girl smiled at me. "We'll make sure they get their ashes," she said.

201

Doña Luz, the matriarch next door, died from congestive heart failure after Easter. The last time I saw her, I took her hand on the sidewalk as Linda cried, and then the EMTs told us to let go and loaded her into an ambulance.

We never saw Mr. Claws again. The pharmacist at the General Hospital didn't have a record of him getting any medications. The social worker from San Mateo County called once more to say he'd been unable to find any other address in his database. Mark and I still make sure to have cash in our pockets just in case, but on Wednesday mornings now we chant the Psalms without Mr. Claws. I suspect he's gone.

The Mission keeps changing. There are shiny apartment buildings going up on the block where the old movie theater used to be, and one of the storefront churches near my house has been replaced by a condominium. And on 24th Street a woman who's just moved to the city carries a new baby in her arms, and slowly begins walking with him across the plaza.

The days grow shorter and then longer; the whole neighborhood goes dry, then greens again with the rains. Every season we remember that we're dust, and to dust we shall return.

Acknowledgments

This book would be impossible without the great editorial and spiritual generosity of Martha Baer, whose abiding love shows me what faith looks like. I'm endlessly grateful to her, to Kate Miles who inspires me, and to my entire family, for their love and support.

Thanks to my neighbors in the Mission, especially the extended Zarate family, including Roberto and Lupe; Robert, Rosalind, Gustavo, Leticia, Lupe, Chino, and Martín; Elissa, Daniel, Kassandra, Sílvia, Gustavo, Raquel, Angélica, and Alejandra. May God bless their lives in this city.

Thanks to Janet Bishop and Thad Povey; David Becker and Renata Martins; Yolanda Campos; Isabel, Lilly, Rogelio and Francisco, for continuing inspiration about what it means to be a neighbor. Thanks to Tani Adams, Gilberto Arriaza and Naomi Roht-Arriaza, Jim and Melinda Jackson, Bob Ostertag, Mark Ritchie, and all who helped me find a home here.

203

Thanks to the people of César Chávez Elementary School and of PODER, for loving the neighborhood so well.

I'm grateful for all who make Church possible, including the people of The Food Pantry, and of St. Gregory of Nyssa Episcopal Church, Holy Innocents Episcopal Church, Advent of Christ the King Episcopal Church, St. John the Evangelist Episcopal Church, Buen Samaritano Episcopal Church, and St. Peter's Catholic Church. My colleagues at St. Gregory's—Paul Fromberg, Sanford Dole, Sylvia Miller-Mutia, and Sherri Lynn Wood—are a joy to work with and generously picked up the slack while I was sequestered away writing. For the sustaining presence of Mark Pritchard and Peggy Graybill at morning prayer, and the occasional lively company of Alexandra Miller-Mutia, I give thanks.

My deepest thanks go to all who allowed themselves to be part of this story, and of my life as it unfolded over the course of writing the book, including Martha Baer, Kevin Callahan, Lupe Castillo, Sanford Dole, Paul Fromberg, George Gibson, Francisco Gonzalez, Cris Gutierrez, Rosa Lee Harden, Will Hocker, Anibal Mejia, Kelsey Menehan, Kate Miles, Bertie Pearson, Francois Pierre, Thad Povey, Mark Pritchard, Julio Rivera, Nancy

Sárraga, Vik Slen, Jeni Schurman Wade, Elizabeth Welch, and Roberto Zarate. Thanks also to Michael Barger, Claire Blackstock, Lawrence Chyall, Cortney Hamilton, Reagan Humber, Lauren Lukason, Noreen O'Brien, John-Michael Reyes, Deb Tullman, and all the others who accompanied me through the streets of the Mission on Ash Wednesday over the years.

Thanks to the friends who offered me space to write, especially Jeff Gaines and John Griffin, Mark Pritchard, and the entire hospitable staff of Bishop's Ranch. I'm grateful to Deb Dwyer and Jane Shaw for reading early drafts and encouraging me; to Martha Baer, Sheryl Fullerton, and Mark Pritchard for their patient and insightful editing; to Nadia Bolz-Weber for her constant support; and to Jim Naughton, Ann Fontaine, and the staff of the Episcopal Café, who helped with my early writings about Ash Wednesday. I'm so happy to have Greg Daniel as my agent and grateful to Wendy Grisham and Chelsea Apple at Hachette for their faith in this book.

Sara Miles
Feast of St. Augustine, 2013

Sara Miles is the founder and director of The Food Pantry, and serves as Director of Ministry at St. Gregory of Nyssa Episcopal Church in San Francisco. Her recent books include *Take This Bread: A Radical Conversion* and *Jesus Freak: Feeding Healing Raising the Dead.*

www.saramiles.net

also by sara miles

Jesus Freak

Take This Bread

How to Hack a Party Line

Native Dancer